Advancing the
Civil Rights Movement

Advancing the Civil Rights Movement

Race and Geography of Life *Magazine's Visual Representation, 1954–1965*

Michael DiBari Jr.

LEXINGTON BOOKS
Lanham • Boulder • New York • London

Published by Lexington Books
An imprint of The Rowman & Littlefield Publishing Group, Inc.
4501 Forbes Boulevard, Suite 200, Lanham, Maryland 20706
www.rowman.com

Unit A, Whitacre Mews, 26-34 Stannary Street, London SE11 4AB

Copyright © 2017 by Lexington Books

All rights reserved. No part of this book may be reproduced in any form or by any electronic or mechanical means, including information storage and retrieval systems, without written permission from the publisher, except by a reviewer who may quote passages in a review.

British Library Cataloguing in Publication Information Available

Library of Congress Cataloging-in-Publication Data Available

ISBN 978-1-4985-3153-5 (cloth : alk. paper)
ISBN 978-1-4985-3154-2 (electronic)

∞™ The paper used in this publication meets the minimum requirements of American National Standard for Information Sciences Permanence of Paper for Printed Library Materials, ANSI/NISO Z39.48-1992.

Printed in the United States of America

For Sherry, Dylan, and Jack

Contents

Acknowledgments ix
List of Images and Figures xi

1. The Power of Photography 1
2. Race, the Media, and *Life* 13
3. Desegregation, Small Communities, and the Photographs of *Life*: 1954 to 1956 33
4. The Little Rock Nine, Sit-Ins, and the Freedom Rides: 1957 to 1962 59
5. Fire Hoses, Police Dogs, and the Civil Rights Act: 1963 to 1965 85
6. *Life* Magazine and the Civil Rights Movement 107

References 119
Index 127
About the Author 133

Acknowledgments

I would like to thank Dr. Joseph Bernt, Prof. Terry Eiler, Dr. Timothy Anderson, and especially Dr. Patrick Washburn for their help, support, and inspiration during the writing of the original dissertation that inspired this book.

Other people who have helped me along the way include: Dr. Aimee Edmondson, Dr. Michael Sweeney, Prof. Stan Alost, Dr. Mavis Carr, and Prof. Wayne Dawkins. A special thank you to my friend and colleague Dr. Ed Simpson, whose help in editing and proofreading was imperative.

I would also like to thank my editor at Lexington Books, Nicolette Amstutz, who gave me the opportunity for the book to be published and assisted me along the way.

Throughout life there are few people who inspire and motivate you. One such person is my mentor, teacher, and friend, Dr. Michael Carlebach. I am a better photographer and a better person because of him.

Finally, my thanks and gratitude to my wife, Sherry, for donating countless hours to proofreading, editing, and discussing this endeavor.

List of Images and Figures

Chapter 1

Image 1.1 Charles Moore's photograph of firefighters spraying water at protesters in Birmingham, Alabama, appeared in *Life*'s May 17, 1963, issue.

Figure 1.1 Stories, pages, and photographs published in *Life* magazine from 1954 to 1965.

Chapter 2

Image 2.1 Gordon Parks photographed Ella Watson in 1942 while working for the Farm Security Administration.

Image 2.2 Gordon Parks photographed Ella Watson at her home with her grandchildren in 1942.

Image 2.3 A photograph of an African-American woman eating watermelon while breast-feeding her child ran at the end of the "Watermelons to Market" story in *Life* magazine on August 9, 1937.

Image 2.4 Margaret Bourke-White's photograph of the 1937 flood in Louisville, Kentucky, appeared in *Life* magazine on February 15, 1937.

Chapter 3

Figure 3.1 Stories, pages, photographs, and letters to the editor published in *Life* magazine from 1954 to 1956.

Image 3.1 A photograph of Roy Bryant and J. W. Milam taken by Edward Clark was published in *Life* on October 3, 1955.

Image 3.2 Robert Kelley's photograph of a mob harassing African Americans as they drove through Clinton, Tennessee, was published in *Life*'s September 17, 1956, issue.

Image 3.3 *Life* published an 1872 lithograph by Currier and Ives, entitled "The Old Plantation Home," on September 3, 1956.

Image 3.4 *Life* ran a photograph of African Americans dancing in Greenville, South Carolina.

Chapter 4

Figure 4.1 Stories, pages, photographs, and letters to the editor published in *Life* magazine from 1957 to 1962.

Image 4.1 Stan Wayman's photograph of Dorothy Counts being harassed by a student at Harding High School in Charlotte, North Carolina, was published in *Life* on September 16, 1957.

Image 4.2 *Life* magazine published Johnny Jenkins' photograph of Hazel Bryan yelling at Elizabeth Eckford on September 16, 1957.

Image 4.3 A photograph of L. Alex Wilson being attacked outside of Central High School in Little Rock, Arkansas, was published in *Life* on October 7, 1957.

Image 4.4 Photographer Malcolm O. Carpenter photographed Ruth E. Tinsley being carried away by two police officers in Richmond, Virginia.

Image 4.5 Charles Moore's photograph of off-duty officers gathering before the riots at the University of Mississippi was published on October 12, 1962, in *Life* magazine.

Chapter 5

Figure 5.1 Stories, pages, photographs, and letters to the editor published in *Life* magazine from 1963 to 1965.

Image 5.1 Charles Moore's photograph of police dogs attacking protesters, published on May 17, 1963, in *Life*, showed passive protesters being attacked.

Image 5.2 After a church bombing in Birmingham, Alabama, *Life* published this simple, yet powerful image of twelve-year-old Sarah Jean Collins in her hospital bed on September 27, 1963.

Image 5.3 Dick De Marisco, of the *New York World Telegraph and Sun*, photographed two police officers beating an African-American man during rioting in Harlem, New York.

Image 5.4 Charles Moore's photograph of the confrontation between Alabama state troopers and marchers on the Edmund Pettus Bridge was published on the cover of *Life*'s March 19, 1965, issue.

ONE
The Power of Photography

Life magazine photojournalist Charles Moore arrived in Birmingham, Alabama, on May 3, 1963. By the time he left the city five days later, he had been arrested, become a fugitive from the law, and shattered the tendons in his ankle.[1] Aside from his own physical reminders of the tumultuous week, he left the nation a lasting legacy of its most violent period since the Civil War. The photographs he took over the five days were some of the most iconic and revealing of the American civil rights movement.[2] They were published as an eleven-page spread in the May 17, 1963, issue of *Life* magazine and left an indelible mark on American society.[3] A year later, the American Society of Magazine Photographers presented Moore with an award for his photographs of events in the South. New York Senator Jacob Javits, who presented Moore with his award, said he believed the photographs coming out of "the struggle for civil rights" that were published in the press and magazines would help to influence the attitudes of the American people and the U.S. Congress. "It is only because pictures backed up the words, no matter how authoritative, that [this injustice] has been credited," he said.[4] In July, Congress finally passed the Civil Rights Act of 1964. Moore's dramatic photographs as well as other images from Birmingham, helped to give equal rights to all U.S. citizens regardless of color.[5]

The Rev. Dr. Martin Luther King Jr. considered Birmingham "the country's chief symbol of racial intolerance."[6] It was a community where human rights had been trampled for so long that "fear and oppression were as thick as the smog from its factories."[7] He and other civil rights leaders hoped to draw attention to the racial inequalities in the city by organizing marches and demonstrations. Although potentially dangerous, they knew that if the media covered the inevitable confrontations between protesters and local authorities, the results had the power to make an impact and change the course of history. Birmingham had the perfect antagonist: Eugene "Bull" Connor, the city's volatile police commissioner.

King knew that dramatic photographs of protesters being beaten had the potential to make an impact on attitudes across the nation.[8] During an early march in Selma, Alabama, he had reprimanded photographer Flip Schulke for not documenting the action. Schulke, a contract photographer for *Life* magazine, had stopped taking photographs and intervened when local white law enforcement officials began shoving black children to the ground. King heard about the incident and told Schulke: "The world doesn't know this happened, because you didn't photograph it. I'm not being cold-blooded about it, but it is so much more important for you to take a picture of us getting beaten up than for you to be another person joining in the fray."[9]

In the days that followed, images of protesters being mauled by police dogs and sprayed by fire hoses appeared in newspapers and news magazines, but when *Life* published the story on May 17, 1963, its effect and impact was stronger than that of any other media outlet.

Gene Roberts and Hank Klibanoff explained in their Pulitzer Prize–winning book, *The Race Beat*, why the impact of Moore's photographs was so powerful: *Life*'s large format and slick paper had "a vivid-

Image 1.1. Charles Moore's photograph of firefighters spraying water at protesters in Birmingham, Alabama, appeared in *Life*'s May 17, 1963, issue. (Photograph courtesy of Black Star Photo Agency.)

ness and sense of enormity that newspapers couldn't touch."[10] Images of white policemen holding snarling police dogs attacking well-dressed African Americans, and firemen using hoses, forcing protesters against buildings, were not only powerful, but also sympathetic and moving. Even more provocative were the letters to the editor three weeks later. Dan Griffin of Anderson, South Carolina, wrote:

> It is such a shame that Negroes who could be out earning money and, in some cases, respect, are participating in such things as the Birmingham violence. They have their own schools. But no, they have to get the white man's school and lunch counter and anything else the white man has made for himself. All they can think about is violence.[11]

The perception that the violence was brought on by the protesters themselves and not white authority was striking, yet not surprising. Audiences took notice. King knew their power. *Life* magazine also knew their power. Images of brutal force against American citizens were not commonly seen in national news magazines and newspapers.

Author Davi Johnson noted the powerful impact that Moore's images had on the nation and abroad in a journal article titled "Martin Luther King Jr.'s 1963 Birmingham Campaign as Image Event." She wrote:

> The Birmingham pictures confronted a nation with visible evidence of its racism, putting before the eyes of the American people irrefutable proof that barbaric practices were not solely the purview of places far away and times long ago, but immediately present. The photos made racism appear repugnant by constructing a dramatic narrative where whites (and the status quo) were identified with vicious animal violence and blacks were codified as brave innocents willing to martyr themselves for justice.[12]

Author and historian Leigh Raiford agreed that the violent images produced in Birmingham were powerful and long lasting. In *Imprisoned in a Luminous Glare: Photography and the African American Freedom Struggle*, she wrote that "these images have shaped and informed the ways scholars, politicians, artists, and everyday people recount, remember, and memorialize the 1960s freedom struggle specifically and movement histories generally." She explained that such images become icons over time and are used in the process of forming our national, racial, and political identity. The frequent use of these powerful images legitimized "the proper place of African Americans within the national imagery" and gives them a "surplus symbolic value."[13]

Life magazine's published images became an integral part in the formation of these ideas across the nation. As early as 1956, two years after the Supreme Court's historic *Brown v. Board of Education* decision that mandated school desegregation, *Life* published a five-issue series of photographs, illustrations, and essays on segregation and its history in America. The magazine had established itself as a national leader in discussing race and racial issues. Its coverage of the conflicts between black and white legitimatized the battle for civil rights and offered stark symbols of an America that many whites refused to acknowledge.[14] Yet, *Life's* coverage did not overtly suggest a righteous crusade. Instead, it presented stories and events as a way to promote a national dialogue and debate on morality, race, and civil rights.

This book examines how *Life* magazine represented the civil rights movement from 1954 to 1965 and helped to frame the debate among America's leaders, policymakers, and readers.

Many scholars have examined the events of the civil rights movement, but none have looked at its visual coverage by one of America's most popular magazines. This book examines all of the images, stories, editorials, and letters to the editor relating to civil rights events, stories, and people in *Life* magazine from 1954 to 1965.

The time period chosen brackets the two seminal events in the nation's struggle to cast off the heavy legacy of segregation: the U.S. Supreme Court decision to end school segregation and the passage of the Voting Rights Act of 1965 by Congress. On May 17, 1954, the U.S. Supreme Court handed down its landmark decision, *Brown v. Board of Education*, which stated that the policy of "separate but equal" with regards to education was invalid. School integration was to become part of America's policy for all people. This marked the beginning of the legitimate and legal battle for civil rights. The study continues through 1965, the

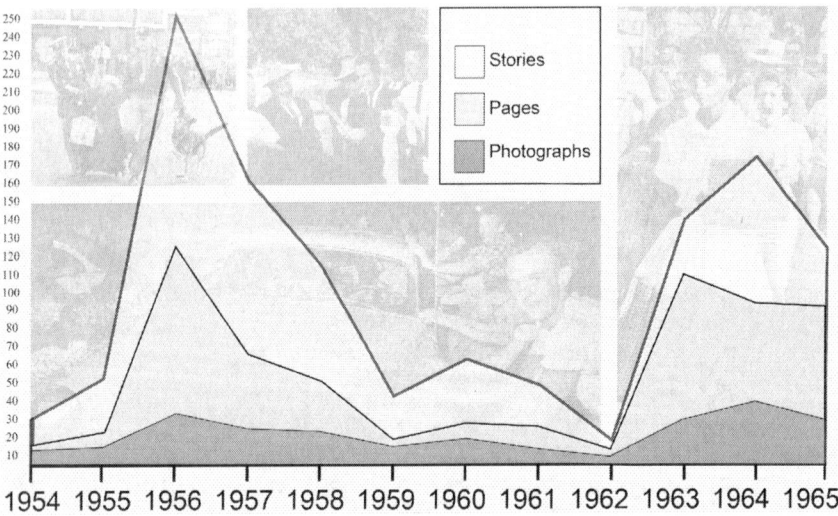

Figure 1.1. Stories, pages, and photographs published in *Life* magazine from 1954 to 1965. (Created by Michael DiBari Jr.)

year that the United States Congress passed the Voting Rights Act prohibiting the use of literacy tests to determine a person's eligibility to vote.

The stories and photographs selected for this study were coded using a content analysis method. The definitions of "civil rights" were defined by the *National Association for the Advancement of Colored People Civil Rights Handbook*.[15] After selecting the published photographs and stories that would be examined, the photographs were analyzed through a method coined by Gillian Rose as "compositional interpretation," which examines images through several components, including content, color, spatial organization, light, and expressive content.[16]

Rose explains compositional interpretation focuses mainly on the "compositionality" of an image, as well as its production. The production of an image takes into account how the image was made, who made it, and its purpose in being made. Rose breaks down the compositionality of an image into content, color, spatial organization, light, and expressive content. Content explains what the image is about, such as firefighters holding a fire hose spaying water at people sitting on a sidewalk; color refers to the hue, the saturation, and the value of the colors in the image; spatial organization refers to lines, shapes, and subject matter within the image; light considers the type of lighting used or the light source within the image; and expressive content refers to emotions, both within the image and the reaction to the image. Because many of these elements are subjective and may have alternate meanings, a thorough understanding of photography is essential.[17] This method was chosen as a place to start the examination process and for its adaptability within the field of geography. This study applies these ideas to the photographs in order to create a framework for interpretation and discussion.

Another important aspect of examining photographs is to consider who created the images, under what circumstances were they created, and who influenced them. In the book *Mediating the Message*: *Theories of Influences on Mass Media Content*, Pamela Shoemaker and Stephen Reese discuss the importance of the producers of media content and why that content should be considered in contemporary research.[18]

This book uses qualitative as well as quantitative methods in addressing and analyzing the production of media content. They include the examination of the papers and memoirs of *Life*'s publisher, Henry Luce, and photographer Gordon Parks; interviews conducted with photographers and editors Steve Schapiro, Art Shay, Jack Corn, Richard Stolley, and Hal Wingo; as well as examination of *Life*'s published articles. These sources, both primary and secondary, provide insight into the decision-making process by editors and photographers in the field with regards to the coverage of civil rights stories.

By using this dual approach, a more comprehensive and thorough analysis of the material can be obtained. Also, the geographic theory of space offers another dimension of research not yet considered. Many of the events and stories covered by *Life* were located in specific areas, such as the southeastern United States. Geography and the idea of the cultural landscape play an important and discernible role in the discourse. Space can be discussed in a physical sense, as well as in a metaphorical sense. The idea of contested space is fundamental when examining the social events during this period. The physical space in each scene, as well as space on the page, can be deconstructed and analyzed with the intent of a greater understanding of the fight for equal space.

Geographer Don Mitchell breaks down space as physical attributes and places where scenes transpire. Space can be a home, a street, a suburban neighborhood, a city block, or a region. It can also be broken up by culture, as in a cultural landscape, which can be examined through many different forms. For instance, types of music, art, or photographs in a magazine can be looked at as a landscape, which can be analyzed and discussed geographically. Mitchell explains that culture can mean many things to many people. It can "signify a 'total way of life' of a people, encompassing language, dress, food habits, music, housing styles, religion, family structures, and, most importantly, values."[19] This study uses the idea of the cultural landscape as the stage on which the stories and photographs published in *Life* magazine become the text. In other words, *Life* becomes its own cultural landscape with its own vernacular and its own visual interpretation.

An example of these geographic ideas can be illustrated by looking at Charles Moore's photograph published on May 17, 1963. Taken from a sidewalk on a downtown Birmingham street, Moore stood behind the firemen who were spraying protesters with fire hoses. The African-American protesters line the sidewalks in small groups, as water from the hose sprays off one of their backs. Their hands and arms are folded around their necks in a protective and nonaggressive manner. The firefighters are photographed from behind leaning forward, spraying their hose as a weapon. The gap between firefighters and protesters is distinct and obvious. There is a clear separation between the two subjects. The space separating the African-American protesters from their aggressors is both literal and figurative. In this one image, *Life* magazine illustrated the aggression and racial divide of the fight for civil rights.

This contention of space can be explained further. James A. Tyner used the concept of geography to theorize black radicalism in his study "Urban Revolutions and the Spaces of Black Radicalism." He described the civil rights movement as a "series of crucial civil, political, social, and economic battles" and defined black radicalism as the remaking of those spaces.[20] He argued black radicals differentiated between "segregated spaces" and "separate spaces," and the solution was not integration but the elimination of segregation. He explained how "white" citizens have the power in society and use it, not only in economic, political, and social contexts, but also in virtually all aspects of life. The "spaces" African

Americans occupy, such as neighborhoods, schools, churches, businesses, and even street corners, are their own. Tyner concluded, "To integrate into a white supremacist society was to negate the spaces of African-Americans," and that the "Black power movement was (and continues to be) about producing space for social justice."[21] Tyner's study looked at these "spaces" in a specific way, calling attention to the struggles and issues of African Americans.

In a 2002 study by David Delaney, race was an important and growing aspect of research. His study, "The Space that Race Makes," looked at "how space works to condition the operation of power and the constitution of rational identities" in regards to race. "Space," he wrote, "may be produced in accordance with ideologies of color-blindness or race consciousness, of integrationism, assimilation, separatism, or nativism."[22] These race-centered ideologies combine with other elements such as "public-private ownership, sexuality, citizenship, democracy, or crime to produce the richly textured, highly variegated, and power-laden spatialities of everyday life." In other words, geography is an ideal field from which to look at these spatial constructs and discourses and apply them to everyday meaning. "Race . . . is what it is and does what it does precisely because of how it is given spatial expression."[23] Delaney also noted that the distribution of power plays an important role in the location, displacement, and relocation of race-making events. These elements "might inform a more critical approach to racial geographies."[24]

"Whiteness" is another approach in looking at the division of space. Steven Hoelscher argued in 2003 that recognizing the past in an idealized way helps to promote and to continue to perpetuate these racist ideals.[25] He described the situation in the small town of Natchez, Mississippi, as the geography of exclusion, that is, "how a dominant group was able to create a culture of segregation that extended well beyond the boundaries of its legal apparatus." The "white" citizens of Natchez, Mississippi, were that "dominant group." He argued that if researchers and historians do not acknowledge that whiteness, it becomes the "norm" and creates an unspoken racism with all other identities as "the other."[26] All of these "discourses" take place in the South, "the main stage on which Americans have played out this fundamental performance of race construction."[27]

LIFE MAGAZINE

During much of the twentieth century, *Life* magazine was one of the most popular weekly, pictorial magazines in the nation. For thirty-six years, from November 1936 to December 1972, its pages were filled with photographs of everyday life from birth to death and war to peace. Its mission, taken from publisher Henry Luce's prospectus for a new magazine, in

1936, was "to see life; to see the world; to eyewitness great events; to watch the faces of the poor and the gestures of the proud; to see strange things . . . to see and to take pleasure in seeing; to see and be amazed; to see and be instructed."[28]

In *The Civil Rights Movement: A Photographic History, 1954–68*, author Steven Kasher explained that during the 1950s and 1960s, one weekly issue of *Life* was "the single most important media organ, seen by more than half the adult population of the United States and reaching more people than any television program."[29] Its circulation in 1954 was about 5.5 million subscribers and grew steadily to more than 7 million by 1965.[30] *Life* had an extremely high "pass-along factor," more than any other mass-circulation magazine. A pass-along factor was the idea that one issue could be read by more than one individual and passed along to others to read. One survey of *Life*'s first year in 1938 indicated a pass-along factor of 17.3, meaning that on average, more than seventeen people read each copy. In early 1965, *Life*'s pass-along factor was estimated at 4.6 persons per copy, giving the magazine an estimated total audience of over 32 million readers.[31]

The magazine was also at the forefront photographically. First, the photographs published in *Life* had a specific "style." In a 2004 article by Andrew Mendelson, style was defined as "particular compositional features that are frequently associated in predictable combinations."[32] *Life*'s first picture editor, Wilson Hicks, described the magazine's style as a unique combination of words and pictures. Each photograph contained a fact, idea, or feeling, bringing a particular point of view to the reader, and each photograph became part of a picture story or photographic essay. Hicks wrote in his 1952 book, *Words and Pictures,* that the magazine used this style to promote its "sense of curiosity, its sense of drama, its sense of history—and its sense of humor" to readers.[33]

Life also created the first, true photographic essay in America.[34] In the 1966 book *Dorothea Lange*, George P. Elliott defined the photographic essay as a "collection of pictures on a single theme, arranged to convey a mood, deliver information, and tell a story in a way that one picture alone can not."[35] Former *Life* editor Maitland Edey described the evolution of the essay as "the emergence of a true partnership among editor, photographer, and designer."[36] In his book *Great Photographic Essays from Life,* he goes on to say that despite this team effort, the photographer was the crucial element.

W. Eugene Smith, Margaret Bourke-White, and Leonard McCombe were a few of the photographers who excelled at producing stories with depth, variety, and humanity.[37] These photographic attributes made the magazine stand out from all other mass circulation magazines and pushed the vernacular of photography into mainstream America.

In *Life's America*, Wendy Kozol examined the pivotal role that *Life* played in the formation and promotion of the American family. She wrote that the magazine's purpose at mid-century was "familiarizing a national audience with visual news and turning Americans into consumers of visual culture through its weekly pictorial view of the world, which accustomed its audience to seeing social life in visual terms."[38] In other words, *Life* codified news images in order to educate and promote visual imagery in society. Its editors envisioned the nation in terms of "the white, middle-class, heterosexual, nuclear family" and played a key role as a producer of postwar culture.[39]

While there is evidence of *Life*'s homogenized middle-class view, this book reveals the magazine, its editors, photographers, and reporters were in the journalistic vanguard of civil rights coverage. For instance, in the six weeks after the integration of Central High School in Little Rock, Arkansas, *Life* devoted thirty-four pages and ninety-five photographs to the event, while *Time* magazine ran twenty-seven photographs on twenty-one pages and *Newsweek* ran twenty-four photographs on twenty pages.[40] This book shows *Life*'s significance as a leading journalistic voice in the debate surrounding civil rights despite its historically Caucasian frame. It helped to establish the issues and paint the movement in stark, moral terms. This can be seen in what events were covered, how they were covered, and how they were placed in the magazine. Over the course of twelve years, *Life*'s photographs and stories brought the struggle for civil rights into America's homes, forcing its audience to confront the realities of segregation. The magazine's editors and photographers believed it could affect people and create change. In the process, it became a symbol, at least for some, of social progress.

EXPLANATION OF CHAPTERS

The structure of this book is both chronological and topical. Chapter 2, "Race, the Media, and *Life*," discusses a brief history of African Americans and race in America. Media coverage of civil rights events by the black press, national news magazines, and *Life* before 1954 is also discussed. The opinions and history of publisher Henry Luce and photographer Gordon Parks are also explored. This chapter sets the stage and places mass media with regards to race in America into context.

Chapter 3 is titled "Desegregation, Small Communities, and the Photographs of *Life*: 1954 to 1956." During these three years, civil rights stories and photographs in *Life* increased each year, culminating in an extensive and informative five-issue series, "Background of Segregation," beginning in September 1956. From the history of slavery in America, life in the Jim Crow South, and then to the current living conditions of African Americans, *Life* took an expansive view of the topic of race and segregation in America.

Chapter 4, "The Little Rock Nine, Sit-ins, and the Freedom Rides: 1957 to 1962," continues with *Life*'s civil rights coverage. During this period, published articles declined to the lowest point of coverage. Some of the events covered were school integration, civil unrest in the South, and the Freedom Rides. The showdown at Little Rock's Central High School between Arkansas Governor Orval Faubus and nine African-American students attempting to integrate produced the most coverage and most dramatic photographs.

Chapter 5, "Fire Hoses, Police Dogs, and the Civil Rights Act: 1963 to 1965," demonstrated *Life*'s coverage of some of the most powerful events in civil rights history. Published stories included the riots at the University of Mississippi; the protests in Birmingham, Alabama; the passage of the civil rights bill; riots in Harlem, New York; the murder of three Freedom Summer volunteers in Philadelphia, Mississippi; and the March on Washington, D.C. These defining events gave fuel to social and political change in American history. The photographs taken and published in *Life* are some of the most iconic and influential of the civil rights movement.

Chapter 6, "*Life* Magazine and the Civil Rights Movement," places events and articles into context and concludes with the magazine's significance with regard to the American civil rights movement. The chapter discusses how *Life* became a catalyst for change and how visual coverage pushed and presented the agenda of civil rights leaders into the public discourse.

Life magazine played a unique and important role in American history. Through its photographs, the magazine showed the world what was happening in the South and in doing so, helped shape the discussion of the American civil rights movement.

NOTES

1. Charles Moore worked as a contract photographer for *Life* through the photography agency Black Star. See Michael S. Durham and Charles Moore, *Powerful Days: The Civil Rights Photography of Charles Moore* (New York: Stewart, Tabori & Chang, 1991), 27–29.

2. Meg Spratt, "When Police Dogs Attacked: Iconic News Photographs and Construction of History, Mythology, and Political Discourse," *American Journalism* 25, no. 2 (Spring 2008): 85–105. See also "They Fight a Fire that Won't Go Out," *Life*, May 17, 1963, 26.

3. Moore's photographs from Birmingham received recognition and an award from the American Society of Magazine Photographers in 1964. He also won the first annual Kodak Crystal Eagle Award in 1989, which is considered one of the most prestigious honors in the industry of documentary photography. See John Kaplan, "The Life Magazine Civil Rights Photography of Charles Moore 1958–1965," *Journalism History* 25, no. 4 (Winter 2000): 138.

4. Jacob Javits was quoted in Vicki Goldberg, *The Power of Photography: How Photographs Changed Our Lives* (New York: Abbeville Press, 1991), 208.

5. See Durham and Moore, *Powerful Days*, 27; Paul Messaris *Visual Persuasion: The Role of Images in Advertising* (Thousand Oaks, California: Sage Publications, 1997), 141,

and Shelley Tougas, *Birmingham 1963: How a Photograph Rallied Civil Rights Support* (North Mankato, Minnesota: Compass Point Books, 2011), 11.

6. Steven Kasher, *The Civil Rights Movement: A Photographic History, 1954–68* (New York: Abbeville Press, 1996), 91.

7. Martin Luther King, *Why We Can't Wait* (New York: New American Library, Signet Books, 1964), 45.

8. See Durham and Moore, *Powerful Days*, 27; and King, *Why We Can't Wait*, 66.

9. Interview with photographer Flip Schulke cited in Gene Roberts and Hank Klibanoff, *The Race Beat: The Press, the Civil Rights Struggle, and the Awakening of a Nation* (New York: Knopf, 2006), 383.

10. Ibid., 322.

11. "Letters to the Editors," *Life*, June 7, 1963, 25.

12. Davi Johnson, "Martin Luther King Jr.'s 1963 Birmingham Campaign as Image Event," *Rhetoric & Public Affairs* 10, 1 (Spring 2007): 1–25.

13. Leigh Raiford, *Imprisoned in a Luminous Glare: Photography and the African American Freedom Struggle* (Chapel Hill: University of North Carolina Press, 2011), 3.

14. See George P. Hunt, "The Racial Crisis and the News Media: An Overview," in Paul L. Fisher and Ralph Lynn Lowenstein, eds., *Race and the News Media* (New York: Praeger, 1967), 14–15.

15. National Association for the Advancement of Colored People, *NAACP Civil Rights Handbook* (New York: National Association for the Advancement of Colored People, 1973), 1. This handbook describes basic programs, policies, and procedures regarding civil rights issues. Chapters are divided into: legal cases, police brutality, criminal cases, housing, education, employment, registration and voting, and boycotts and direct action campaigns. These headings make logical categories, which will be applied to the stories and photographs published in *Life* magazine.

16. Gillian Rose, *Visual Methodologies: An Introduction to Researching with Visual Materials* (Thousand Oaks, California: Sage, 2012), 51. "Compositional interpretation" is a manufactured term that Rose uses as an approach to break down and examine the content of an image.

17. As a professional editorial and newspaper photographer for more than eighteen years, my experience has been helpful informing and guiding this study.

18. Pamela J. Shoemaker and Stephen D. Reese, *Mediating the Message: Theories of Influences on Mass Media Content*, 2nd ed. (White Plains, New York.: Longman, 1996).

19. Don Mitchell, *Cultural Geography: A Critical Introduction* (Oxford, England: Blackwell Publishers, 2000), 13.

20. Katherine McKittrick and Clyde Adrian Woods, eds., *Black Geographies and the Politics of Place* (Toronto, Ontario: South End Press, 2007), 219.

21. Ibid., 225.

22. David Delaney, "The Space that Race Makes," *The Professional Geographer* 54(1) (2002): 7.

23. Ibid.

24. Ibid.

25. Steven Hoelscher, "Making Place, Making Race: Performances of Whiteness in the Jim Crow South," *Annals of the Association of American Geographers* 93(3) (2003): 659.

26. Ibid., 662.

27. Ibid., 657.

28. Erika Lee Doss, ed., *Looking at Life Magazine* (Washington, D.C.: Smithsonian Institution Press, 2001), 2. See also Henry Luce, "A Prospectus for a New Magazine," at www.life.com/image/92925995, accessed November 2010.

29. Kasher, *The Civil Rights Movement*, 13.

30. A. J. Zuilen, *The Life Cycle of Magazines: A Historical Study of the Decline and Fall of the General Interest Mass Audience Magazine in the United States during the Period 1946–1972* (Uithoorn, Netherlands: Graduate Press, 1977), 89, 99.

31. Ibid.

32. Andrew Mendelson, "Slice-of-Life Moments as Visual 'Truth'" *Journalism History* 29, 4 (Winter 2004): 166–178.

33. Wilson Hicks, *Words and Pictures* (New York: Arno Press, 1973), 42–45. Hicks began as picture editor in 1937, three months after *Life*'s first issue, and was executive editor from 1939 to 1952. "Wilson Hicks, a Former Editor of *Life* Magazine, Dies at 73," *The New York Times*, July 7, 1970, 38.

34. Some European magazines, such as the *Berliner Illustrierte Zeitung*, the *Illustrated London News*, and *Vu* developed the photographic essay in the late 1920s and early 1930s. See Alan Brinkley, *The Publisher: Henry Luce and His American Century* (New York: Alfred A. Knopf, 2010), 209.

35. George P. Elliott, *Dorothea Lange: Catalog of Exhibition* (New York: Doubleday, Museum of Modern Art, 1966), 278.

36. Maitland Edey, *Great Photographic Essays from* Life (Boston: New York Graphic Society, Little, Brown and Company, 1978), 20.

37. Ibid.

38. Wendy Kozol, Life*'s America: Family and Nation in Postwar Photojournalism* (Philadelphia: Temple University Press, 1994), 185.

39. Ibid., ix.

40. The author examined issues of *Time* and *Newsweek* magazines on microfilm from September 16, 1957, to October 21, 1957, the same time frame as *Life*. The issues were September 16, September 23, September 30, October 7, October 14, and October 21 for both *Time* and *Newsweek*.

TWO
Race, the Media, and *Life*

In 1942, Gordon Parks photographed Ella Watson, a cleaning lady for the Farm Security Administration (FSA). This iconic photograph brought dignity to a race of people at a time when they barely had a voice. The image, known as "American Gothic," depicted Watson holding a mop and broom in front of the American flag. The dramatically lit portrait was Parks' attempt to put a face on poverty and became the beginning of his fight against the evils of racism.[1] In his book *Moments Without Proper Names*, Parks wrote, "It is the heart, not the eye, that should determine the content of the photograph."[2]

American Gothic marked the beginning of Parks' photographic style, that is, the use of deliberate and dramatic lighting. The light, in this case, served to separate the "figure from the everyday, [and] at the same time, pose, clothing, and props seem to underscore the sitter's essential character," a character depicting grace and poise.[3]

In 1941, Parks received a grant from the Julius Rosenwald Fund,[4] which provided him the opportunity to work and train under Roy Emerson Stryker of the Farm Security Administration in Washington, D.C. The FSA was part of President Franklin D. Roosevelt's New Deal designed during the Great Depression to help stop rural poverty. Under Stryker's guidance, the FSA produced thousands of documentary-style images of Americans dealing with the hardships of daily life. The *Maryland Historical* magazine described the photographs taken during this time as "vividly [portraying] the despair and poverty found in depression-struck rural areas—the haggard migrants, dustbowls, shanties, and sharecroppers. But they also depicted the strength of the people, the beauty of the land, and the stark simplicity of life in the Thirties."[5]

In early January 1942, Parks spent much of his first day at the FSA exploring Washington, D.C. Stryker had told him to familiarize himself

Image 2.1. Gordon Parks photographed Ella Watson in 1942 while working for the Farm Security Administration. (Photograph courtesy of the Library of Congress, Prints & Photographs Division, FSA/OWI Collection, ref. number LC-USF34-013407-C.)

with the city. He told Parks to "go to a picture show, a department store, eat in restaurants and drugstores. Get to know this place."[6] By the time he returned to the office at the end of the day, he had been refused service at a drugstore breakfast counter, a movie theater, and a department store, where he had been unable to purchase a winter coat. He was angry, frustrated, and yearned to photograph the racism that he had just experienced. Stryker told him to think about what he had experienced and write down his ideas about how to fight prejudice. "Think in terms of images and words. They can be mighty powerful when they are fitted together properly," he said.[7]

When Parks met Watson in the same building he worked in, she recounted her life's story. It was a "pitiful" one, he later recollected. Her mother had died when she was a young girl, and a lynch mob had killed her father. She married after high school and became pregnant. Her husband was accidentally shot and killed two days before their daughter was born. Years later, her teenaged daughter gave birth to two illegitimate children and died weeks after the birth of the second child. The grandchildren had to be watched by different neighbors while Watson worked during the day. It had been a difficult life.[8]

After Watson told her story, Parks asked to photograph her in front of the flag. Under Stryker's guidance and suggestion, he also photographed her at her home and at church.

As he experienced racism and poverty through her life, he gained knowledge, confidence, and versatility as a photographer.[9] He later wrote in his memoir about the experience: "I have known poverty firsthand, but there I had learned how to fight its evil—along with the evil of racism—with a camera."[10]

Photographs from Parks and other photographers in the FSA were used throughout the country in newspapers, magazines, and books as well as displayed in museums. Stryker believed that publishing the photographs of Americans in all aspects of life "reduced social distances between classes, races, and regions."[11] Since publishers and editors did not have to pay for the rights to reproduce the photographs, they were used extensively. Sherwood Anderson used FSA photographs in his 1940 book, *Home Town*, and Richard Wright used them to illustrate his 1941 book, *12 Million Black Voices*, just to name a few.[12] Some of the photographs published in Wright's book depicted African-American children in horrific conditions: sleeping on blankets on floors or in rusted cots or reading in a kitchen with newspapers covering the walls and table.[13] These types of images were more commonplace than Parks' dignified portrait of Watson.

Although some critics believed the photographs produced by the FSA to be political propaganda, most agreed that the images were indicative of the times.[14]

Image 2.2. Gordon Parks photographed Ella Watson at her home with her grandchildren in 1942. (Photograph courtesy of the Library of Congress, Prints & Photographs Division, FSA/OWI Collection, ref. number LC-USF34-013404-C.)

The conditions of African Americans during the first half of the twentieth century were abysmal. Life had not changed much since Reconstruction, the period after the Civil War, and in many cases, it had gotten worse for African Americans.

RACIAL CONDITIONS IN THE UNITED STATES

In 1944, Swedish researcher Gunnar Myrdal published a two-volume book titled *An American Dilemma: The Negro Problem and Modern Democracy*, which explored the plight and condition of the "Negro in America." He noted that the status of the "Negro" had been rising since the 1870s but at an incredibly slow pace.[15] He concluded this era of stagnation was ending, and there was reason to "anticipate fundamental changes in American race relations, changes which will involve a development toward American ideals."[16] That change would be accelerated with the beginning of World War II and would be radically influenced by compelling and dramatic photographs.

In the United States, the population of African Americans had grown seventeen times by 1940 in comparison to 1790, the year that the first census was taken. However, during the same period, the population of whites had increased thirty-seven times.[17] During this time, most African Americans lived in the South with Louisiana, Mississippi, Alabama, Georgia, South Carolina, North Carolina, and Florida having the highest density.[18] By the first part of the twentieth century, the legal status of African Americans had been solidified with "Jim Crow laws" and by the landmark 1896 Supreme Court decision, *Plessy v. Ferguson*. Jim Crow laws referred to laws that racially segregated or separated on the basis of race.[19] This was basically legal discrimination, and although African Americans were entitled to the "equal benefit of all laws," southern whites, in particular, used this legal friction to promote the idea of "separate but equal."[20]

The *Plessy v. Ferguson* decision pitted Homer Adolph Plessy against the East Louisiana Railroad Company. Plessy, an African-American man who looked white, was arrested for not moving to the "colored" car of a train after purchasing a first-class ticket in the white section. His lineage had both African-American and white great-grandparents and, in his particular case, seven white great-grandparents and one African-American great-grandparent. By a seven-to-one decision, the Supreme Court ruled in favor of the railroad company, firmly establishing the "separate but equal" policy.[21] This doctrine stipulated that separation of the races was perfectly legal and permissible as long as African Americans were provided with "substantially equal facilities."[22] In segregated states, which were mainly in the South, nearly all aspects of life were separated, from schools and buses to lunch counters and department stores to parks and golf courses; even the smallest and most insignificant activities, such as drinking fountains and bathrooms, were separate. In *The Race Beat: The Press, the Civil Rights Struggle, and the Awakening of a Nation*, authors Gene Roberts and Hank Klibanoff wrote why southerners defended segregation, explaining that "it represented the best way to hold on to what they had. Segregation was the essence of life in the South. It was the rock."[23]

This separation was not purely physical. In the book *Remembering Jim Crow: African Americans Tell about Life in the Segregated South*, Jim Crow was described as "not merely about the physical separation of blacks and whites." Nor was segregation about laws. "In order to maintain dominance, whites needed more than the statutes and signs that specified 'whites' and 'blacks' only; they had to assert and reiterate black inferiority with every word and gesture, in every aspect of both public and private life."[24]

Grace Elizabeth Hale wrote in *Making Whiteness: The Culture of Segregation in the South, 1890–1940*, about how southern whites not only promoted white supremacy but enforced and lived by it. She argued that the "culture of segregation turned the entire South into a theater of racial difference, a minstrel show writ large upon the land."[25] White southerners used these ideas to help promote "black" inferiority. "African Americans were inferior because they were excluded from the white spaces of the franchise, the jury, and political officeholding," she wrote. They lived in inferior homes, attended inferior schools, and held inferior jobs. And, most importantly, they were portrayed as inferior in public spaces, such as waiting rooms, restrooms, theaters, restaurants, and seats on a bus. Segregation and discrimination created "class exploitation, disempowerment, and racial privilege."[26]

Geographer Don Mitchell breaks down space as physical attributes or places where scenes transpire. Space can be a home, a street, a suburban neighborhood, a city block, or a region. It also can be broken up by culture, as in a cultural landscape, which can be examined through many different forms. Mitchell explained that culture can mean many things to many people. It can "signify a 'total way of life' of a people, encompassing language, dress, food habits, music, housing styles, religion, family structures, and, most importantly, value."[27] The term "culture" can be an elusive and complex idea.[28] In this case, culture, as in cultural landscape, refers to the photographs and layouts in *Life* magazine as representative of events that transpired in the civil rights movement. In other words, the pages of *Life* magazine become a stage or landscape upon which the fight for equal rights takes place.

As James Tyner explained, "Geography, as the study of space, is well positioned to contribute to an understanding of racism and other forms of injustice." It is concerned with the "forwarding of 'alternative' geographies, of transformed spaces."[29]

Racism and discrimination had clung to every aspect of public and cultural life in the United States in the years leading up to World War II; but, as Myrdal noted, "race relations are bound to change considerably."[30]

THE BLACK PRESS

In 1942, about the same time that Parks was photographing Watson in Washington, D.C., an African-American newspaper, the *Pittsburgh Courier*, had just begun its famous "Double V Campaign." The Double V, which stood for victory overseas in the war as well as victory over racism and discrimination in the United States, became a national campaign in the fight for equal rights.[31] As part of the black press, the *Pittsburgh Courier* used its unique voice and influence to help bring about the change that Myrdal noted.

Myrdal wrote that the importance of the black press was in the "formation of Negro opinion, for the functioning of all other Negro institutions, for Negro leadership and concerted action." It was used as an educational tool, and it determined the "special direction of the process through which the Negroes [were] becoming acculturated."[32] The first African-American newspaper, *Freedom's Journal*, was published in New York City in March 1827. Charles A. Simmons wrote in 1998 about its philosophy and goal of delivering messages of unity to its readers with "passion and emotion, and [to] let white editors and citizens know that black citizens were humans who were being treated unjustly."[33] Because of the injustices that African Americans had to endure, it was not surprising that black newspapers in the United States pushed for more rights during World War II, which helped set in motion the civil rights movement in the 1950s.[34]

Historian Patrick S. Washburn argued in *The African American Newspaper: Voice of Freedom*, that by using a "powerful and compelling form of advocacy journalism rather than the standard objective style found in most white-owned newspapers," the black press became a conduit for those who pushed for civil rights. He does not suggest, however, that the black press caused the civil rights era but that the newspapers were instrumental in its outcome.[35]

Washburn explained that beginning in 1910, circulation of black newspapers began to increase while illiteracy rates for African Americans began to decline. During this time, one newspaper owner adopted a model "that would change black newspapers forever."[36] In 1905, Robert Abbott, founder of the *Chicago Defender*, decided to model his paper after the sensational yellow journalism that other publishers, such as William Randolph Hearst and Joseph Pulitzer, popularized in the late 1890s. "Yellow journalism" was a term used to describe reporting that propagated crime news, sex and scandal, misfortune and sports stories.[37] Its over-sized headlines, abundant use of photographs and illustrations, and liberal reporting of the news are still employed in many supermarket tabloids of today.[38] The *Defender* would not be objective in its stories but would become advocates for the African-American race.[39] It was in this climate of journalism that the Double V campaign made its impact.

The *Pittsburgh Courier* began its Double V campaign when it published a letter by James G. Thompson on January 31, 1942, which suggested advocating for a double victory: the first V for "victory over our enemies from without, [and] the second V for victory over our enemies from within."[40] Washburn argued that Thompson's letter might have been the "most famous ever run by a black paper" because it inspired other black newspapers to push for a "double victory."[41] Soon, African Americans across the country were pushing for equal rights, especially in the military. Newspaper articles and editorials were critical of the U.S. government and the war. This did not go unnoticed by the Justice Department or Military Intelligence, and after the threat of espionage and sedition eased, the government relaxed its policies regarding many issues concerning African Americans and black newspapers.[42]

The black press made two important gains for African Americans during the war. The first was a February 1944 meeting between President Franklin D. Roosevelt and the Negro Newspaper Publishers Association. It was the first time a sitting president met with a such a prominent group of African Americans at the same time; and the second was when African-American reporters were finally able to attend presidential press conferences.[43] After playing an integral part in war coverage, the black press went on to play an equally important role in covering civil rights events and issues throughout the United States.

THE NATIONAL MEDIA AND RACE

Although the national media did not play as persuasive a role as the black press in covering race and racial issues, it did play an important role. In the book *The White Press and Black America*, Carolyn Martindale reported the results of a content analysis study of African-American coverage in four major newspapers: *The Atlanta Constitution*, *The New York Times*, *The Chicago Tribune*, and *The Boston Globe*. She examined 245 issues regarding stereotypical images, everyday life, civil rights, and minority life throughout three specific time periods, 1950–53, 1963–68, and 1972–80. The results of her study indicated that during the 1950s, little coverage of African American–related stories were found in the four newspapers. As little as 1 to 2 percent of available news space was devoted to such stories. Coverage increased and peaked in the 1960s but then declined in the 1970s. She attributed the increase in the 1960s to the activities of the civil rights movement, legislation for those rights, riots, and journalists' own increased awareness of African-American lives and, perhaps, a desire to cover them more accurately than they had in the past.[44]

In a related study examining national magazines during a similar time period, Paul Lester and Ron Smith found similar results. They examined sample issues of *Life*, *Newsweek*, and *Time* magazines from 1937 to 1988, counting the pictorial representation of African Americans in each year. On the pages devoted to photographs, 3.36 percent contained pictures of African Americans during the fifty-one-year period. This was an increase in coverage over time. Lester and Smith concluded this was due to a "sensitivity on the part of editors to show African Americans as equal members of society" and not to protests, entertainment, or sports.[45]

Life *Magazine*

For thirty-five years, *Life* magazine covered social, political, and breaking news issues through photographs and words. In the book *Life's America*, Wendy Kozol described it as "one of the most popular American magazines in the twentieth century and the most important picture magazine of its day."[46]

In a 1983 study of the African-American community in Life magazine, Mary Alice Sentman examined fifty-two issues from 1937 to 1972. Her premise was that magazines "not only reflect the values of society, but also serve as an important socializing force."[47] Life's founder and publisher, Henry R. Luce, understood this idea well. He wrote in his 1936 prospectus that the magazine's purpose was "To see life; to see the world; to eyewitness great events . . . to see and to take pleasure in seeing; to see and be amazed; to see and be instructed."[48]

In Sentman's study, images of African Americans were categorized into basic divisions, such as crime, entertainment, and sports. Her research concluded that coverage and visibility of African Americans increased over the years, but, ultimately, Life had missed an opportunity to show African Americans in everyday life situations or as everyday citizens. By today's standards, many of Life's early stories and photographs depicted them in racist and stereotypical manners.[49]

One example of this was the story "Watermelons to Harvest," published on August 9, 1937. The issue's cover featured an African-American male from behind sitting on a wooden cart loaded with watermelons. The unidentified shirtless and faceless man heads down a dirt path between crops. His pants and suspenders are tattered and frayed.

In the book *Everything Was Better in America: Print Culture in the Great Depression,* author David Welky wrote, "Life's customary response to America's 'minority problem' was to ignore it."[50] When Life did publish photographs of African Americans, they were portrayed as "comic devices."[51] This can be seen in the last two photographs of the watermelon story. The first image depicts an African-American woman eating an enormous wedge of watermelon while nursing her baby.

> Nothing makes a Negro's mouth water like a luscious, fresh-picked melon. Any colored "mammy" can hold a huge slice in one hand while holding her offspring in the other. Since the watermelon is 92% water, tremendous quantities can be eaten. What melons the Negroes do not consume will find favor with the pigs.[52]

Referring to the last image in the story, which showed pigs devouring watermelons, Welky noted that the comparison and placement of the two images was degrading, insulting, and another stereotypical example of life.[53]

Author Erika Lee Doss also wrote that Life's representation of African Americans during its first decade was "meager and abysmal, like most of mainstream media."[54] One example was in an April 19, 1937, article on Huddie Ledbetter, better known as "Lead Belly." The article, subtitled "Bad Nigger Makes Good Minstrel," featured a full-page color photograph of the musician, wearing overalls, with no shoes and sitting on

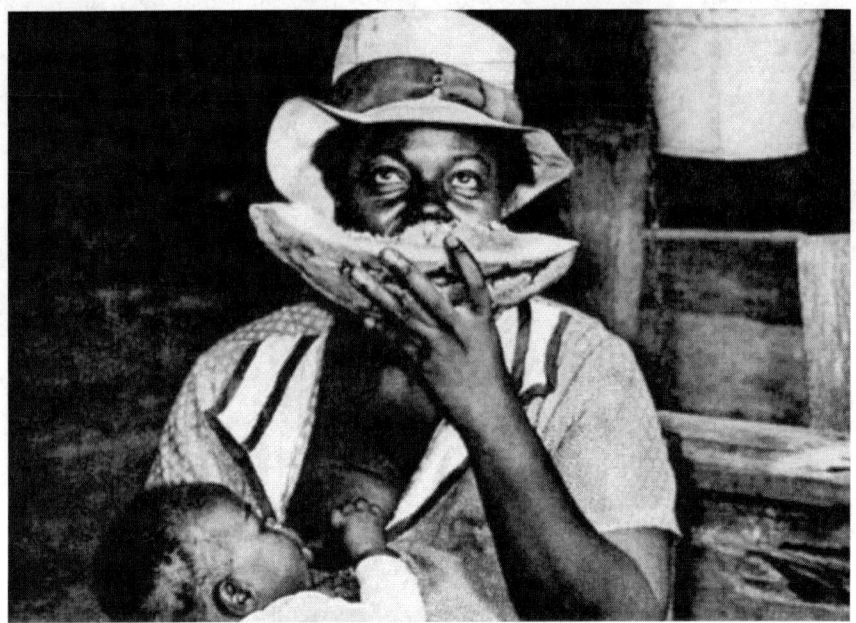

Image 2.3. A photograph of an African-American woman eating watermelon while breast-feeding her child ran at the end of the "Watermelons to Market" story in *Life* magazine on August 9, 1937. Freelance photographer A. P. Burgert took the image. (Photograph courtesy of the Burgert family.)

canvas bales while strumming his guitar. The caption informed readers that Ledbetter called himself "De King Of De Twelve-String Guitar Players Of De Worl."⁵⁵ One year later, when *Life* published "Negroes, The U.S. Also Has a Minority Problem," Doss pointed out how the magazine "reified racist as stereotypes by captioning one photograph of a group of African-American stevedores with 'tote dat barge, lift dat bale' and by describing a shot of black crapshooters as 'Baby needs new shoes.'"⁵⁶ Despite a 1944 editorial, "Negro Rights," in which Luce used "impassioned rhetoric about black's rights," Doss noted the fact that "throughout the war the magazine continued to print pictures of blacks as lessers suggests its hesitancy about actually visualizing American racial justice, or its lack of knowledge about how to do so."⁵⁷

This opinion may be true as a generalization of *Life*'s early imagery of African Americans, but is not exclusive or the case in every instance. Dolores Flamiano argued in 2009 that there were examples of "exceptional photographs [which] exposed racial injustice and showed the dignity and humanity of black people."⁵⁸ A photograph in *Life* by Margaret Bourke-White, during the aftermath of a 1937 flood in Louisville, Kentucky, was one such example.

The image depicted a group of African-American men, women, and children lined up for food from the Red Cross, standing in front of a large billboard created by the National Association of Manufacturers.[59] The billboard featured a smiling white family driving a car with the words, "There's no way like the American Way" and "World's Highest Standard of Living."

Flamiano wrote, "For today's viewers, it is difficult not to interpret this juxtaposition as an indictment of America's economic and racial inequalities. Yet the image is ambiguous enough to leave room for diverse responses, from outrage to irony to patriotism."[60] Bourke-White's photograph was not humorous or demeaning to African Americans, although it did not show them in a positive light. The victims waiting in line were well dressed and stoic. In the book *A Staggering Revolution: A Cultural History of Thirties Photography*, John Raeburn wrote that this particular photograph simultaneously evoked an "economic inequality and racial discrimination."[61] Although it represented an incident during a specific natural disaster, one *Life* reader recognized that it transcended this illustrative purpose. Louis Stoumen of Bethlehem, Pennsylvania, wrote that Bourke-White was "a truly great photographer, and, in exhibiting the

Image 2.4. Margaret Bourke-White's photograph of the 1937 flood in Louisville, Kentucky, appeared in *Life* magazine on February 15, 1937. (Photograph courtesy of Getty Images.)

editorial courage to print her photographic social comment," *Life* had distinguished itself as a remarkable picture magazine.[62] Flamiano concluded her analysis of the Louisville flood photograph by calling Bourke-White's "contribution to African American representations in photojournalism significant and lasting."[63]

As noted earlier, another important racially charged article for *Life* was "Negroes, The U.S. Also Has a Minority Problem," published on October 3, 1938. The twelve-page spread covered poor southern African Americans as well as higher educated "black" society.[64] As Doss pointed out, some of the captions promoted racist stereotypes and were a missed opportunity for *Life*. "Claiming journalistic objectivity and ignoring its own role in framing the black subject, *Life* smugly wrote that the 'Negro is probably the most social and gregarious person in America.'"[65]

The two largest photographs in the opening spread of the article were portraits by *Life* staff photographer Alfred Eisenstaedt: a close-up of a young African-American woman singing and an older African-American man dressed in a suit looking disheveled. Flamiano noted that the photographs might be eye-catching, but their meanings were changed by captions that cast a lurid light on both the young woman and the old man.[66] The first caption read:

> In the Congo jungle, a black girl like this would be moaning a murky tribal chant. This girl is at church in the South, singing the plain music of a Baptist hymn as no white girl could sing it and as its own composer could never have imagined it. As she sings, with her eyes half-closed, her ecstatic face becomes the face of the American Negro finding in music and in religion his soul's two great consolations.

The caption for the older man's portrait on the following page also was condescending, calling him an "old 'darky' who has borrowed trappings, bearing and beard of the Southern colonel and thus created a caricature of his old massa."[67] Flamiano noted both of these captions "transform two otherwise pleasing portraits of dignified individuals into crude and dehumanizing racial clichés."[68]

During this time, captions and text that appeared in the magazine were scripted and controlled by the editor. *Life* editor Wilson Hicks wrote that the picture editor had enormous power and influence: "His preferences and prejudices, together with his publication's policies, which he understands and interprets, exert a vital influence on the ultimate product. . . . The editor is the selector and integrator not only of words and pictures, but of ideas and points of view as well."[69]

The 1938 article continued with a brief, straightforward overview of African-American life from the slave trade to rural, southern farmhands working in fields, to education and ballet, to up-and-coming artists and high society, to business leaders. The essay covered a broad spectrum of talented people and country club–type activities. The content of the stories and images "reveals the complexity and ambivalence of *Life*'s racial ideology, as well as the cultural impact of the Harlem Renaissance."[70] Welky, again in *Everything Was Better in America: Print Culture in the Great Depression*, also pointed out this conundrum. He noted musician Duke Ellington "hailed [the article] as 'one of the fairest and most comprehensive articles ever to appear in a national publication.'" However, not everyone agreed. Dr. P. N. Charbonnet of Tulsa wrote in a letter to the editor, "I have become increasingly irritated and disgusted at the very evident 'nigger-loving' proclivities of your editorial board."[71] Welky pointed out how "Charbonnet's anger crystallized the magazine's dilemma. No matter how progressive it wanted to be, *Life* still needed to satisfy a varied group of readers, the majority of whom were neither black nor desirous of true black equality."[72]

Another noteworthy story and the first major essay about an African American was Gordon Parks' "Harlem Gang Leader," published on November 1, 1948. Flamiano noted this story "represented a step forward for racial representation in mainstream magazines because it moved beyond one-dimensional black stereotypes to provide a portrait of an individual,"[73] although it was about a gang leader. The nine-page story featured the life of seventeen-year-old Leonard "Red" Jackson, the leader of the Midtowners, a Harlem gang. Parks pitched the story to *Life*'s picture editor, Wilson Hicks, during their first meeting together; and, reluctantly, he responded with "the incredibly low offer of two hundred dollars to do the entire story." Parks agreed to photograph the story only after Hicks offered an "unlimited expense account."[74]

The photographs of Red depicted everyday scenes of gang life: hanging out with gang members, painting bikes, and spending time with his family. In one photograph, "Red holds ball of yarn while his mother listens to the radio and knits a table mat."[75] The images became more dramatic as the story progressed with a photograph of Red and Herbie Levy leaning over an open casket, studying the "wounds on the face of Maurice Gaines, a buddy of theirs who was found dying one night on a Harlem sidewalk." The article ended on a disheartening image of Red, silhouetted, as he walked down an empty street with the caption, "After being paraded around in style as Harlem's 'boy mayor,' Red walks 25 blocks home alone. He has few people he can turn to for sincere help."[76]

Author Erika Doss explained that this story marked a turning point in terms of racial representation for *Life*. She wrote that Red's story was a "postwar paean to social responsibility, a liberal call addressing the needs of black urban poor and, especially, black male youth."[77] Many of *Life*'s readers agreed. Frank W. Carr of Waukesha, Wisconsin, wrote, "*Life*'s presentation of the Red Jackson story was, I think, the best sociological study of your magazine's career. The last statement made the whole article." Shirley Cohen of New York added, "I for one have made up my mind to try to help boys like Red Jackson and members of his gang become somebodies [sic]. . . . I am further going to dedicate myself to this cause." And finally, Thomas Robinson of Pittsburgh, Pennsylvania, wrote, "As a fellow boy, I hope that the people who are seriously and practically interested will get out and do something about it."[78] Doss pointed out that previous letters in the magazine regarding the coverage of juvenile delinquency "have not drawn these sorts of letters, which suggests that response to this 1948 article lay with its difference and, in particular, the compelling character of its photographs."[79]

The transformation of African-American imagery in the media during the first half of the twentieth century was evident. Flamiano concluded in her study that there had been a renaissance in the field of documentary photography. With photographers such as Bourke-White, Parks, and Alfred Eisenstaedt paving the way as social reform photojournalists, the portrayal of African-American life continued to gain in coverage and in stature.[80] Although it was not evident from early portrayals, *Life*'s publisher, Henry R. Luce, substantial role in this evolution.

Life's Publisher, Henry R. Luce

Henry Robinson Luce was one of the most prolific publishers and editors of the twentieth century.[81] He was co-founder of what became the largest and most influential magazine empire in America, launching *Time*, *Fortune*, *Life*, and *Sports Illustrated*.[82] Author Robert E. Herzstein described him as "the greatest journalistic innovator of his century and a dedicated patriot during some of the most turbulent times in our history."[83] Even before the first issue of *Life* was published, Luce had an understanding of the African-American dilemma. Hertstein described him as having "great personal sympathy for the black cause, for he, too, had grown up surrounded by an oppressed people of a different race." He believed that "preventing other people from pursuing happiness was . . . a sin."[84] Luce was born in China on April 3, 1898, to missionary parents, Elizabeth Root Luce and Henry Winters Luce. According to Hertstein, there were two forces which helped influence his character and worldview. The first was his Protestant Christianity upbringing and the second was a "fervent faith in America's God-ordained global mission in Asia."[85] These forces followed him throughout his career. Former reporter and editor Richard B. Stolley explained: "*Life* could not have taken the stance it had on segregation without Luce approving it. Luce paid very close attention [and] was politically aware."[86]

The first issue of *Life* was published on November 23, 1936, and quickly became one of America's most popular news magazines. In 1937, the end of its first full year, the magazine ran a three-million-dollar deficit. But by 1939, with advertising rates substantially higher, *Life*'s circulation had reached more than two million. Writing about *Life*'s explosive circulation, author Erika Doss noted by the late 1940s, *Life* reached "21 percent of the entire population over ten years old" (around 22.5 million people) and took in 19 percent of every magazine advertising dollar in the country.[87] Author David Halberstam described it this way:

> The birth of *Life* reflected Luce at his best. He had envisioned the magazine as it would be, and he had pushed his printers hard for the production techniques that would make *Life* possible. Equally important, he had not faltered when the very success of *Life* threatened to bring down his entire company. His editorial instincts always took precedence over any cautionary sense of the bottom line.[88]

Life stood out from other magazines for many reasons. First, it had its own writing style, clear and concise prose, which was very different from that of *Time*, Luce's other magazine. Second, they treated photographs with respect and dignity; that is to say, they did not crop them into strange or unusual shapes as other magazines tended to do at the time. Luce and his editors spent months contemplating and agonizing over "finding the right look" for their fledgling publication. They wanted the photographs to dominate its pages and also wanted to create a visual vernacular.[89] They understood that readers wanted more than to just flip through a picture magazine. The editors wanted to visually educate its readers. They did this by running photo stories and photo essays. In the book *Truth Needs No Ally*, author and *Life* picture editor Howard Chapnick described the "photographic essay" as photographs tied together by a single theme so that its structure and sequence create a narrative style that could tell a "full-blown coherent story."[90]

Luce's opinions and style of "cultural reportage" were not without their critics. Historian James L. Baughman pointed out examples of how *Life*'s tone in stories was written with "finality" for many academic issues. The magazine would include stories on high art along with features of "horses on roller skates," which "only denied readers the power to discriminate between high and mass culture, creating a mindless 'midcult.'"[91] *Time* magazine also drew criticisms for its political prejudices and editorializing. Luce had no problem with his magazines' editorial content reflecting his opinions. This was seen in *Time*'s bias toward entering World War II and in *Life*'s coverage of the war.[92]

In the book *Luce and His Empire*, W. A. Swanberg wrote that because of the high circulation of both *Time* and *Life* magazines, Luce's "opinion, message, point of view or slant . . . would be likely to reach at least a third and perhaps considerably more of the total literate adult population of the country."[93] Swanberg speculated that because of this enormous leverage in shaping public opinion, and perhaps in a "move aimed at blocking criticism before it became serious," Luce established and financed the Commission of Inquiry on Freedom of the Press.[94] The commission, which concluded in 1947, was led by the president of the University of

Chicago and Luce's friend, Robert M. Hutchins. It called on newspapers to be more "'socially responsible' to all elements of a community."[95]

A year after the commission's results were published and with a new sense of social responsibility, Luce turned his energy inward at America to address race relations. During a speech he gave at a meeting for the Inter-Racial Fellowship General Assembly of the Presbyterian Church, in Seattle, Washington, he said, "The position of Negroes in American life must be rapidly improved. Discrimination against Negroes must be radically lessened. The political rights of Negroes must be unambiguously assured. Equality of opportunity for Negroes must be more fully realized."[96] He argued there were three basic reasons for better race relations in America: economic, patriotic, and moral. Regarding the economic argument, Luce stated: "We will all be better off if all Negroes are given equality of opportunity to work and serve to the fullest of their capacity in all walks of life. It makes hard-boiled economic sense to say that by keeping millions of Negroes down, we lose at least $4,000,000,000 a year. American Negroes should be earning . . . much more than we are now able to save."[97]

Luce's second reason for improving race relations was the "American argument," also called the "patriotic argument—that is, our country has a very special immediate need of good race relations and if a man truly loves his country, he will be sensitive to the needs of this country. . . . America is the most wonderful country that ever was. But there's a stain on the American flag—the stain of discrimination. We've got to get that stain out of the flag and keep it out."[98] His third reason for better race relations was "simply because it is the right thing to do and wrong not to." He concluded that there is a need for "congregations of much greater diversity—rich and poor, thinkers and doers, workmen and professional men, artists and shopkeepers, white and colored."[99]

These ideas remained with Luce throughout the 1950s, but it was not until 1954 when two major events in American history brought the plight of African Americans to the forefront of the public discourse. First, the Supreme Court decision of *Brown v. Board of Education* profoundly and legally changed the way Americans dealt with segregation. And second was the murder of Emmett Till, a fourteen-year-old African-American boy who was lynched in Money, Mississippi. A photograph of Till's mutilated body appeared in the September 15, 1955, issue of *Jet* magazine. Many historians and researchers alike, including Paul Hendrickson, Juan Williams, and Davis W. Houck, believe this was the beginning of the modern civil rights movement.[100]

African-American journalist Simeon Booker covered the Till trial for *Jet* magazine. He described the publication as a "galvanizing moment." He recalled, "I know of no one who after seeing that photograph in *Jet*, ever forgot it—from Rosa Parks who said [she] thought of Emmett Till when she refused to give up her seat in Montgomery a few months later to the young activists who descended on Mississippi for the Freedom Summer in 1964."[101]

Life, Luce's premiere photographic magazine, had covered both events, helping to bring the struggle for equality into American homes and into the public discourse.

NOTES

1. Gordon Parks, *To Smile in Autumn: A Memoir* (Minneapolis: University of Minnesota Press, 2009), 24.
2. Gordon Parks, *Moments Without Proper Names* (New York: Viking Press, 1975), 7.
3. Gordon Parks, *Bare Witness: Photographs by Gordon Parks* (Stanford, California: Iris & B. Gerald Cantor Center for Visual Arts at Stanford University, 2006), 9.
4. The $2,000 Julius Rosenwald award was offered between 1917 and 1948 by Julius Rosenwald, the Chicago-based heir to the Sears, Roebuck fortune. The award was given to African Americans and white southerners who wished to work on problems in the South or those who expected to have a career in the South. Gordon Parks was the first photographer to receive the award. See Parks, *Bare Witness*, 13.
5. See dust jacket of F. Jack Hurley, *Portrait of a Decade: Roy Stryker and the Development of Documentary Photography in the Thirties* (Baton Rouge: Louisiana State University Press, 1972).
6. Gordon Parks, *A Choice of Weapons* (New York: Harper & Row, 1966), 222.
7. Ibid., 227.
8. Ibid., 230–231.
9. Parks, *Bare Witness*, 15.
10. Parks, *To Smile in Autumn*, 24.
11. Colleen McDannell, *Picturing Faith: Photography and the Great Depression* (New Haven, Connecticut: Yale University Press, 2004), 9.
12. Ibid. See also Sherwood Anderson, *Home Town* (New York: Alliance Book Corp, 1940); and Wright and Rosskam, *12 Million Black Voices*.
13. Wright and Rosskam, *12 Million Black Voices*, 57, 80, 84, 107.
14. McDannell, *Picturing Faith*, 9.
15. See Gunnar Myrdal, *An American Dilemma: The Negro Problem and Modern Democracy* (New York: Harper & Row, 1962); and Gunnar Myrdal, "The Racial Crisis in Perspective," in Armistead Scott Pride and Jack Lyle, *The Black American and the Press* (Los Angeles: W. Ritchie Press, 1968), 6.
16. Pride and Lyle, *The Black American*, 6.
17. Myrdal, *An American Dilemma*, 157, 397.
18. Ibid., 184.
19. John La Farge, *The Race Question and the Negro: A Study of the Catholic Doctrine on Interracial Justice* (New York, Toronto: Longmans, Green and Co., 1943), 152.
20. Myrdal, *An American Dilemma*, 191.
21. Patrick Scott Washburn, *The African American Newspaper: Voice of Freedom* (Evanston, Illinois: Northwestern University Press, 2006), 39–42.
22. Gene Roberts and Hank Klibanoff, *The Race Beat: The Press, the Civil Rights Struggle, and the Awakening of a Nation* (New York: Knopf, 2006), 9.
23. Ibid., 37.
24. William Henry Chafe, Raymond Gavins, and Robert Rodgers Korstad, *Remembering Jim Crow: African Americans Tell about Life in the Segregated South* (New York: New Press, in association with Lyndhurst Books of the Center for Documentary Studies of Duke University, 2001), 1.
25. Grace Elizabeth Hale, *Making Whiteness: The Culture of Segregation in the South, 1890–1940* (New York: Pantheon Books, 1998), 284.
26. Ibid., 285.

27. Don Mitchell, *Cultural Geography: A Critical Introduction* (Oxford: Blackwell Publishers, 2000), 13.

28. Anthropologist Bronislaw Malinowski stated that culture "comprises [of] inherited artifacts, goods, technical processes, ideas, habits and values." Raymond Firth, ed., *Man and Culture: An Evaluation of the Work of Bronislaw Malinowski* (London: Routledge & Kegan Paul, 1957), 16. Clifford Geertz described the concept of culture believing that "man is an animal suspended in webs of significance he himself has spun." He believed culture to be those "webs." Clifford Geertz, *The Interpretation of Cultures: Selected Essays* (New York: Basic Books, Inc., 1973), 5. Kroeber and KluckhoIn identified more than 150 definitions of culture. Alfred L. Kroeber and Clyde Kluckholn, *Culture: A Critical Review of Concepts and Definitions*, Papers, Peabody Museum of Archaeology & Ethnology, Harvard University, Vol. 47(1), 1952, 223.

29. James Tyner, *The Geography of Malcolm X: Black Radicalism and the Remaking of American Space* (New York: Routledge, 2006), 5–8.

30. Myrdal, *An American Dilemma*, 1022.

31. Washburn, *The African American Newspaper*, 143.

32. Myrdal, *An American Dilemma*, 923.

33. Charles A. Simmons, *The African American Press: A History of News Coverage during National Crises, with Special Reference to Four Black Newspapers, 1827–1965* (Jefferson, North Carolina: McFarland & Co., 1998), 5.

34. Washburn, *The African American Newspaper*, 8.

35. Ibid.

36. Ibid., 82–83.

37. Frank Luther Mott, *American Journalism: A History, 1690–1960*, 3rd ed. (New York: The MacMillan Company, 1962), 539.

38. Shirley Biagi, *Media/Impact: An Introduction to Mass Media* (Belmont, California: Thomson Wadsworth, 2007), 57.

39. Washburn, *The African American Newspaper*, 84.

40. See James G. Thompson's letter to the editor in the *Pittsburgh Courier*, January 31, 1942, cited in Washburn, *The African American Newspaper*, 143–144.

41. Ibid.

42. U.S. Attorney General Francis Biddle met with publisher John Sengstacke of the *Chicago Defender* in 1942 to discuss charges of sedition and espionage. This resulted in a "toning down" of articles criticizing the U.S. war effort. See ibid., 154–158.

43. Ibid., 172–173.

44. Carolyn Martindale, *The White Press and Black America* (New York: Greenwood Press, 1986), 79–82.

45. Paul Lester and Ron Smith, "African-American Photo Coverage in *Life*, *Newsweek* and *Time*, 1937–1988," *Journalism Quarterly* 67 (Spring, 1990): 136.

46. Kozol, *Life's America: Family and Nation in Postwar Photojournalism* (Philadelphia: Temple University Press, 1994), viii.

47. Mary Alice Sentman, "Black and White: Disparity in Coverage by *Life* Magazine from 1937 to 1972," *Journalism Quarterly* 60, no. 3 (1983): 501.

48. David Edward Scherman, *The Best of Life* (New York: Flare Books, 1975).

49. Sentman, "Black and White," 508.

50. David Welky, *Everything Was Better in America: Print Culture in the Great Depression* (Urbana: University of Illinois Press, 2008), 106.

51. Ibid.

52. "Watermelons to Harvest," *Life*, August 3, 1936, 52.

53. Welky, *Everything Was Better in America*, 106.

54. Erika Lee Doss, "Visualizing Black America: Gordon Parks at *Life*, 1948–1971," in Erika Lee Doss, ed., *Looking at Life Magazine* (Washington, D.C.: Smithsonian Institution Press, 2001), 229.

55. "Lead Belly: Bad Nigger Makes Good Minstrel," *Life*, April 19, 1937, 39.

56. Doss, *Looking at Life Magazine*, 229; See also "Negroes, The U.S. Also Has a Minority Problem," *Life*, October 3, 1938, 48.

57. Doss, *Looking at* Life *Magazine*, 229.
58. Dolores Flamiano, "African Americans in *Life*, 1936–1948: From Sensational Racism to Civil Rights," paper delivered at the annual American Journalism Historians Association Convention, Birmingham, Alabama, 2009, 6.
59. "The Flood Leaves Its Victims on the Bread Line," *Life*, February 15, 1937, 9.
60. Flamiano, "African Americans in *Life*, 1936–1948," 7.
61. John A. Raeburn, *A Staggering Revolution: A Cultural History of Thirties Photography* (Chicago: University of Illinois Press, 2006), 210–211.
62. "Letters to the Editors," *Life*, March 1, 1937, 68.
63. Flamiano, "African Americans in *Life* 1936–1948," 13.
64. "Negroes, The U.S. Also Has a Minority Problem," *Life*, October 3, 1938, 48–59.
65. Doss, *Looking at* Life *Magazine*, 229.
66. Flamiano, "African Americans in *Life* 1936–1948," 14.
67. "Negroes, The U.S. Also Has a Minority Problem," *Life*, October 3, 1938, 49.
68. Flamiano, "African Americans in *Life* 1936–1948," 15.
69. Wilson Hicks, *Words and Pictures* (New York: Arno Press, 1973), 48.
70. Ibid.
71. "Letters to the Editors," *Life*, October 24, 1938, 2.
72. Welky, *Everything Was Better in America*, 105–106.
73. Flamiano, "African Americans in *Life* 1936–1948," 21.
74. Parks, *To Smile in Autumn*, 35–36.
75. "Harlem Gang Leader," *Life*, November 1, 1948, 98–99.
76. Ibid., 106.
77. Doss, *Looking at* Life *Magazine*, 221–223.
78. "Letters to the Editors," *Life*, November 22, 1948, 19–20.
79. Doss, *Looking at* Life *Magazine*, 223.
80. Flamiano, "African Americans in *Life* 1936–1948," 24–25.
81. See Alan Brinkley, *The Publisher: Henry Luce and His American Century* (New York: Alfred A. Knope, 2010), xii ("In the middle years of the twentieth century . . . the Luce magazines were the most successful, popular, and influential of them all."); and Robert Edwin Herzstein, *Henry R. Luce: A Political Portrait of the Man Who Created the American Century* (New York: C. Scribner's Sons, 1994), 12.
82. Brinkley, *The Publisher*, ix.
83. Robert Edwin Herzstein, *Henry R. Luce,* Time, *and the American Crusade in Asia* (Cambridge, UK: Cambridge University Press, 2005), 1.
84. Herzstein, *Luce: A Political Portrait*, 88.
85. Ibid., 1.
86. Telephone interview, Richard B. Stolley, December 30, 2010. Stolley worked for *Life* from 1953 until its demise in 1972. He worked in the Atlanta bureau from 1956 to 1960 and was the Los Angeles bureau chief from 1961 to 1965. He also worked as the Washington bureau chief and as the senior editor for editorial coverage in Europe.
87. Doss, *Looking at* Life *Magazine*, 2–3.
88. David Halberstam, *The Powers That Be* (New York: Knopf, 1979), 64.
89. Brinkley, *The Publisher*, 215.
90. Howard Chapnick, *Truth Needs No Ally: Inside Photojournalism* (Columbia: University of Missouri Press, 1994).
91. James L. Baughman, *Henry R. Luce and the Rise of the American News Media* (Boston: Twayne Publishers, 1987), 172.
92. Ibid.
93. W. A. Swanberg, *Luce and His Empire* (New York: Scribner, 1972), 214.
94. Ibid.
95. Ibid.
96. "Speech at meeting for Inter-Racial Fellowship General Assembly of the Presbyterian Church U.S.A., Seattle, Washington," May 30, 1948, Henry Robinson Luce Collection, box 73, folder 5, page 2, Library of Congress, Washington, D.C.
97. Ibid., 3.

98. Ibid.

99. Ibid., 5.

100. There are numerous studies regarding the civil rights movement that began in 1954. A few of them are: Paul Hendrickson, *Sons of Mississippi: A Story of Race and Its Legacy* (New York: Alfred A. Knopf, 2003); Belinda Robnett, "African-American Women in the Civil Rights Movement, 1954–1965: Gender, Leadership, and Micromobilization," *American Journal of Sociology* 101, no. 6 (1996): 1661; Juan Williams, *Eyes on the Prize: America's Civil Rights Years, 1954–1965* (New York: Viking, 1987); and Davis W. Houck and David E. Dixon, *Rhetoric, Religion and the Civil Rights Movement, 1954–1965*, Vol. 1 (Waco, Texas: Baylor University Press, 2006).

101. E. James West, "We Were All Pioneers: A Discussion with Simeon Booker," *Southern Quarterly* 52, no. 1 (Fall, 2014): 215–223.

THREE

Desegregation, Small Communities, and the Photographs of *Life*: 1954 to 1956

In July 1955, *Life* magazine published a story about a small rural school that integrated a year after the Supreme Court's famous *Brown v. Board of Education* decision. The three-page story, "A Morally Right Decision," included ten photographs of young African Americans on their first day of elementary school in Hoxie, Arkansas, a small farming community in the northeast corner of the state.[1] Just days after the story was published, local residents in Hoxie protested the decision of the school board to integrate the schools and called for the resignation of its members. The elementary school closed two weeks early as a result.[2]

The Supreme Court's decision did not specify a date for schools to be desegregated. But according to a *New York Times Magazine* article two months after the *Life* article was published, the Hoxie School Board decided that by integrating sooner rather than later, "It could save the cost of operating the one Negro school and a salary of its teacher . . . [and] the tuition and transportation costs of eight Negro high school students it would have to send to Jonesboro," the nearest local African-American high school twenty-three miles away.[3] The *Times* article by Cabell Phillips stated that the issue of *Life* containing the Hoxie story "was passed [among local residents] as eagerly from hand to hand as a $3 bill would be."[4] Phillips wrote that it "seems fairly certain that the article not only triggered the latent discontent in Hoxie but also stirred up the white supremacy forces elsewhere as well."[5] The reaction to *Life*'s article was immediate. In *Framing the South: Hollywood, Television, and Race during the Civil Rights Struggle*, Allison Graham described a meeting of residents at city hall, where "angry townspeople waved the *Life* article about and made speeches calling for a school boycott."[6] The townspeople picketed the school and petitioned for the resignation of school board members, who refused to rescind their decision.[7]

The ten black-and-white photographs, taken by Gordon Tenney of the photography agency Black Star, seemed innocuous enough. The opening image depicted six African-American students standing together against a brick wall as several white students milled about.[8] The caption stated, "Children of Negro cotton farmers timidly await a teacher's instructions to register for school."[9] The expressions on the children's faces were those of apprehension and nervousness. In contrast, the final photograph in the story showed two African-American girls walking arm in arm with two white girls. The expressions on three of the girls' faces were jovial and happy (the fourth girl was looking down). One reader, E. Lewis Dahl of Farmville, interpreted the photograph differently.[10] In a letter to the editor, he wrote that Peggy, the white student, looked frightened and pathetic.[11]

The three-page article followed the simple narrative of new students attending a new school. The photographs showed what they actually looked like, and the text helped to explain and give depth to their meaning. The space in and around the African-American students also played a part in the telling of the story. The new students in the opening image were physically separated from the other white students, almost invisible to them. As the story progressed, they appeared closer to each other, and by the end of the photographic essay, the students were arm in arm. *Life* not only showed and explained to viewers the story, but visually described integration within the photographs themselves, thus normalizing the process. For viewers, the ability to see students getting along and parents "showing concern" but ultimately accepting the new students, described a non-violent solution.

The Hoxie, Arkansas, package was among the forty-six civil rights stories published in *Life* from 1954 through 1956. In 1954, six stories were published covering twelve and a half pages; in 1955, ten stories were published on twenty-three pages; and, in 1956, thirty stories were published covering 125 pages. These three years were grouped together because of the steep increase in coverage, which peaked in 1956 and declined in 1957.

This study adopted its definition of civil rights from the National Association for the Advancement of Colored People's *Civil Rights Handbook*.[12]

The stories over the three years included reaction to the 1954 Supreme Court *Brown v. Board of Education* decision, the integration of the Hoxie Elementary School in Arkansas, the lynching of Emmett Till in 1955, and a five-issue series on segregation beginning in September 1956. An analysis of the stories revealed that they covered three broad issues: social, moral, and political. These issues will be discussed over the next three

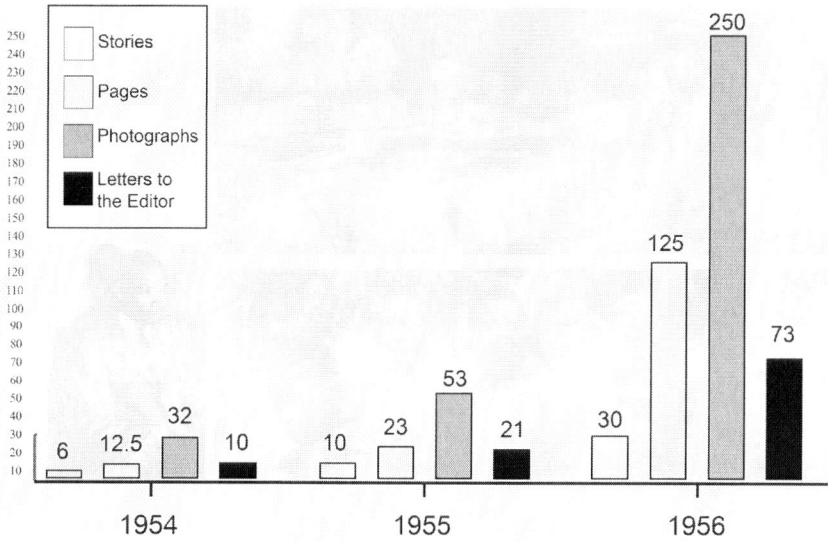

Figure 3.1. Stories, pages, photographs, and letters to the editor published in *Life* magazine from 1954 to 1956. (Created by Michael DiBari Jr.)

chapters, showing how *Life* and its editors presented each story. The photographs are discussed and examined in terms of Gillian Rose's visual methodology: production and composition. Production refers to who photographed the image, such as a staff photographer, contract photographer, or freelance photographer. In most cases, this can be determined by looking at the contents page in each magazine. Who produced each photograph and story became increasingly important, as coverage of events intensified over the years and more than one photographer was sent to cover the same event. When *Life* sent a staff photographer to cover an event, they invested time and resources on its coverage. This would also indicate the importance of the story. Composition included content, color, spatial organization, light, and expressive content.[13] The deconstruction of the photographs helped to inform the geographic idea of landscape and the contention of space, which will be discussed throughout the next three chapters.

1954: *BROWN V. BOARD OF EDUCATION*

In 1954, the Supreme Court handed down a decision in the landmark case *Brown v. Board of Education*. This important decision would be the basis of protests, marches, legal maneuvers, and violence in the years to come. *Life* published a story about it in May. Not only was it the magazine's most significant story that year; it was also one of the country's most important.

On May 31, 1954, two weeks after the Supreme Court's unanimous decision in *Brown v. Board of Education*, *Life* published "A Historic Decision for Equality," explaining that the decision would affect the lives of millions of Americans.[14] In the 1998 book *The Civil Rights Movement*, Peter Levy wrote that although the decision was a "key moment in the history of the civil rights movement, putting the law of the land on the side of those who sought to eradicate racial inequality, the decision signaled only the beginning of the modern civil rights movement, not its culmination."[15] The ruling on May 17, 1954, stated, "separate educational facilities are inherently unequal," and made it clear that the 1896 *Plessy v. Ferguson* decision upholding segregation had been overturned.[16] The Supreme Court's decision was on five desegregation cases from Delaware to Kansas, which had been consolidated into one. The story in *Life* featured photographs of the five African-American children named in the case and described their situations.[17] All of the photographs in the article were published in black-and-white. In contrast to the portraits of the students, *Life* ran a photograph on the opposite page of Herman Talmadge, the governor of Georgia. The caption described him as a "diehard defender of segregation" and suggested that he would consider converting all of Georgia's public schools to private in order to avoid the court's decision.[18]

The following two pages showed six photographs from Orangeburg, South Carolina, a small "prosperous and moderately progressive community of 15,322."[19] One photograph was of young, well-dressed, African-American children dancing at a May Day party. The children attended Christ the King parochial school. Another photograph on the same page depicted a group of white first graders from Mellichamp Elementary School lining up to play. The expressions in both images were very different from each other. The African-American children had serious and focused expressions on their faces as they held hands and danced, while the white children smiled and laughed as they lined up in front of their school.[20] The tone of each photograph's expressive content could not be more dissimilar: the first was of concentration and determination, and the second one was of cheeriness and merriment. Both images, taken by staff photographer Robert W. Kelley, directly correlated with society's attitudes toward the larger issue of racial discontent.

In another image on the same page, a clear distinction and separation was made between white children and African-American children. The photograph, also taken by Kelley, was photographed from inside a school bus looking past the silhouetted heads of white students as African-American students walk by. A majority of the image's composition was of the inside of the bus with only a small part showing the students outside. The caption stated that both white and "Negro children" have fourteen buses each, "but Negro [buses were] more crowded."[21] The physical separation between the students on the bus and the students outside the bus spoke to the divide in attitudes on education, especially in the South. The photographs composition visually builds on the argument of the divide still present in education.

In the final two spreads of the story, *Life* added historical context to the Supreme Court's decision by writing about the first school segregation case in 1849, *Roberts v. the City of Boston*, and the "separate but equal" doctrine from the 1896 *Plessy v. Ferguson* decision. The article ended on a positive note as *Life* noted that two states, Delaware and Kansas, had already begun the process of integration in their schools. The accompanying photographs also were positive in nature. One showed Myrtha Trotter, an African-American student who was allowed to attend a Claymont, Delaware, high school after a state court ruled, "Negro facilities were unequal." The image depicted Trotter smiling broadly with her arms folded in front of Claymont High School as white students filled the scene behind her.[22]

The story's final photograph depicted a crowded classroom at the Randolph School in Topeka, Kansas. Jacqueline Womack, an African-American student was shown sitting at a desk in the foreground, listening and sharing a book with another unidentified, white student. The other students in the background of the photograph work intently with books open and pencils in hand. The teacher was shown talking to students in the last row while standing in front of a wall of student-made art. The caption read that while the Supreme Court was making its decision, "Last September, while its case was before court, Topeka voted to abolish elementary school segregation under Kansas' local option clause."[23]

Although the photograph did not contain expressive content in the faces of the students, it did evoke a sense of seriousness and normalcy in a school setting. Womack was part of the class: not only was she physically sitting in the class, she interacted with a white student in a studious manner.[24] The minimal space between them visually pointed out how students from different races can work together in harmony.

Life presented the story by putting faces and names onto the Supreme Court's decision. Brown and the other children named in the court proceedings were talked about as people, not in the technical jargon of a legal court battle. They were young students with personalities. Harry Briggs Jr. was a "polite, eager boy who wants to become a preacher when he grows up." Linda Brown was a "bright eyed" eleven-year-old who was "forbidden to attend a white elementary school five blocks from her home."[25] *Life* also had ended the story on a positive note with two examples of schools that had already integrated, thus normalizing a contentious situation. By publishing spaces that had been occupied by white students and now integrated, *Life* took a stand whether intentional or not.

"A Reason for Smiles in 'Back-of-Town,'" published on March 29, 1954, was about a new African-American school in New Orleans, Louisiana. The article described how "Back-of-Town" meant "a worn-out section inhabited by Negro families with an ever-growing number of children," but because of the opening of the new elementary school, the children "had something to smile about." The article, framed as a broader social issue, also pointed out that the school was the first one that had been built in New Orleans in the past thirteen years.[26]

On May 31, 1954, *Life* published an editorial to coincide with its coverage of the Supreme Court's *Brown v. Board of Education* decision. "A Head Start on Racial Equality" described how the nation could follow President Dwight Eisenhower's political lead in dealing with civil rights issues. The president, who had made many African-American political appointments, did not act with a political motive "but more from the deep-seated moral and spiritual convictions" of his beliefs. The editorial offered many political examples within the government and ended on a moral note:

> We are all in the midst of a gigantic historical undertaking, the perfection of racial equality, which will require the whole of America's great political talent. Patience and mutual accommodation will be needed, but so will firmness and a rooted belief in the righteousness of the goal. Of all these qualities, the White House is setting an example for the nation.[27]

The final article related to civil rights in 1954 was an editorial, "The 'Whys' of Hate," which staunchly defended integration. The article made the point that prejudice was a learned trait and that, hopefully, over time, each "new American [generation] will be less prejudiced than the proceeding one." It also noted that segregation was morally wrong, and thus, it framed the article as a moral issue.[28]

1955: LYNCHING AND HOXIE, ARKANSAS

In 1955, *Life* published ten articles related to civil rights. The articles included stories about "The Family of Man" exhibition at the Museum of Modern Art, African-American slums in Chicago, NAACP lawyer Thurgood Marshall, the integration of Hoxie Elementary School, and the murder of Emmett Till and subsequent trial. The events of 1955 had fueled and propelled African Americans into action.

The first civil rights–related article in 1955 began with the same topic as it had ended the year: a lynching. "Common Bonds of Man" was published on February 14, 1955. The article coincided with a photography exhibit, curated by photographer Edward Steichen, which displayed a photograph of an African-American man chained to a tree. The year ended with several articles about the murder of Till.

The Museum of Modern Art exhibition, titled "The Family of Man," brought together 503 photographs by 273 photographers from sixty-eight countries and was proclaimed by *Life* as "the most ambitious photographic exhibition ever held."[29] The photographs depicted scenes, portraits, and moments of everyday life from around the world. According to Eric J. Sandeen in *Picturing an Exhibition*, "the main source [of photographs] for the exhibition turned out to be the *Life* magazine files." Wayne Miller, Steichen's assistant, spent more than seven months searching through more than 3.5 million images in *Life*'s archives.[30] In 1999, Monique Berlier wrote in *Picturing the Past: Media, History, and Photography* that the exhibit and accompanying book "reinforced the commonality of life and epitomized the goodness of human beings around the world" but also was criticized for its "superficiality, lack of contextualization, vagueness, and inability to bear the weight of history, as well as for the sentimentality of its theme."[31] One of the most disturbing photographs from the exhibition was an image of a "lynched black man chained to a tree." Steichen removed the photograph after the first week, disliking the attention from visitors and the press.[32] In a 1984 interview, Miller said, "This violent picture might become a focal point . . . that people [and the press] would focus on that and . . . would miss the point, the theme of the show being interrupted by this individual photograph . . . so we removed it for that purpose, not because we didn't think it important, but the presentation of material was dissonant to the composition."[33] It was also missing from the accompanying book but was included in *Life*'s twelve-page spread promoting the historic show.

The photograph was simple yet graphic. It depicted a shirtless African-American man tied to a tree with a chain around his neck and his lower back. His arms were shown tethered by a rope while being pulled away from his body from somewhere outside of the frame. The figure was slumped against a tree, alone in a wooded area. The caption read "Death Slump at Mississippi Lynching (1937)."[34]

In contrast to this disturbing image, published on the facing page, was a vague and ambiguous photograph labeled "Playtime Torment in Chicago Park." It depicted a young, white girl with her hands tied to a tree. Because of the tight cropping, it is hard to distinguish or extract any other information from the image. Both photographs depicted individuals with hands tied.

The third photograph in the spread, captioned "Son's Rebellious Fury on Connecticut Lawn," showed a young boy holding a piece of wood above his head while a woman, most likely his mother, attempted to take it away. The fourth image in the spread, captioned "Panic as Communists Approach Shanghai," showed a crowd of people tightly packed together looking anxious and nervous. Of the four photographs in the spread, the image of the dead African American was the most violent.[35]

The "Death Slump" photograph was first published in *Life* on April 26, 1937, without giving credit to a photographer. The caption under the image stated, "A frightful example of lynching occurred while the House was debating. At Duck Hill, Mississippi, two Negroes accused of murdering a white man were tortured with a blowtorch and lynched. The one shown above was 'Bootjack' McDaniel."[36] The caption referred to a debate in Congress over the Gavagan anti-lynching bill in April 1937. The bill passed in the House of Representatives but then died in the Senate.[37]

The fact that *Life* published the disturbing photograph was significant. Because the exhibition opened on January 26, 1955, and the issue of *Life* was dated February 14, the editors of *Life* might not have had enough time to switch out the image.[38] In addition, it had only been eight months since the Supreme Court's *Brown v. Board of Education* decision and, according to former *Life* reporter and editor Richard B. Stolley:

> Racial matters were on journalists' minds, especially at *Life*; I suspect plans were already underway for the multi-part series on segregation that appeared in *Life* the next year. [The magazine] never ducked running sensational pictures, especially if they involved news stories rather than celebrities. . . . And finally, my own explanation, which is that "The Family of Man" was so sweet and uplifting, that it must have seemed proper to inject some reality into American life back then.[39]

The following article, "An Encroaching Menace" on April 11, 1955, described slum growth in Chicago. The problem was largely, although not entirely, an African-American problem. *Life* reported that hundreds of migrants reached the city each month creating the crisis. The story was presented as a social issue within the context of city life but ended offering a solution with "urban renewal."[40]

On June 20, 1955, *Life* published an article about the oratory arguments in the Mississippi governor's race and quoted the racially charged rhetoric from the candidates. Ross Barnett, who won the election and became the governor, was quoted as calling the Supreme Court's *Brown v. Board of Education* decision "wrong legally, morally and spiritually."[41] Five of the six images accompanying the story were close-up portraits of each candidate, photographed from a low angle, which made each of them look unattractive and sinister. Charles E. Swann of Jackson, Mississippi, noted in a letter to the editor that the photographs chosen made the candidates look like "backwoods revivalists."[42] Bill Scribner of Drumright, Oklahoma, pointed out that the article and photographs reminded him of Germany's Adolf Hitler.[43] Both letters indicated at least two readers noticed how photographs could have an influence on viewers.

The article about the Hoxie integration ran in July 1955 followed by four articles covering the Till murder and trial.

Emmett Louis Till, a fourteen-year-old African-American youth from Chicago was visiting relatives in Money, Mississippi, in late August 1955 when he was brutally murdered by Roy Bryant and his half-brother, J. W. Milam. In *Sons of Mississippi: A Story of Race and Its Legacy*, Paul Hendrickson explained that Till had reputedly whistled at Bryant's wife, Carolyn, made lewd advances, and grabbed her during a visit to the grocery and meat market that the Bryants owned. His mutilated body was found in the Tallahatchie River three days later.[44] The first photograph *Life* ran about the murder on September 12, 1955, was of Till's mother, Mrs. Mamie Bradley, reacting to her son's coffin. Till's body had been shipped to Chicago from Mississippi for viewing and burial.[45]

On October 3, 1955, *Life* published three pages covering the trial, which was held in an adjoining county in the town of Sumner. The first two pages consisted of courtroom sketches of the proceedings drawn by the prolific freelance illustrator Franklin McMahon. Although the story described the trial, it was framed as a fight against prejudice in Mississippi. "Emmett Till's Day in Court" began with a description of the small courtroom in the Mississippi Delta and how the state was intently trying to convict two white men for the brutal murder of a "Negro" boy for whistling at one of the men's wife. The prosecution would be up against a huge concentration of Mississippi prejudice.[46]

After the opening spread of illustrations, a page of photographs from the trial by *Life* staff photographer Edward Clark accompanied the article. They depicted the defendants in the courtroom before and after the trial, as well as scenes around Money, Mississippi. Two photographs in particular were significant because they represented the sentiment of many southerners. The first showed J. W. Milam before the trial with his wife and two sons sitting in the courtroom. He was light-heartedly talking to his two shirtless, young sons. The composition of the image showed a courtroom scene with all white faces sitting behind the defendants as Milam and his wife waited for the trial to begin. Their facial expressions were playful, relaxed, and not typical for a man on trial for murder.

The second photograph was taken after the proceedings. Its caption read, "After acquittal Bryant and Milam lit cigars and posed proudly with their wives." The photograph, taken on an angle and slightly from above, depicted the two defendants with their wives. Milam was grinning broadly with a cigar in his mouth and his arm draped around his wife as she leaned into him. Bryant was pictured with his wife, sitting beside the couple in a similar pose, smiling and relaxed. The expression and tone in the photograph was one of lightheartedness, pride, and relaxation.[47] All the photographs and illustrations in the article were published in black-and-white. Clark, the photographer, was able to isolate the two couples so that no other person was recognizable in the photograph. This was done by tightly cropping on the two couples, which drew readers' attention to the expressive content of the defendants.[48]

The crop was most likely done by an editor.

Image 3.1. *Life* published a photograph of Roy Bryant (top) and J. W. Milam on October 3, 1955, taken by Edward Clark. The caption read that the defendants "lit cigars and posed proudly with their wives" after being acquitted for the murder of Emmett Till. (Photograph courtesy of Getty Images.)

The body language, expressions, and mannerisms of the defendants could be compared to the attitudes and opinions of many southerners during the mid-1950s. The article pointed out the undertones of "racial hatred" in the case when "the defense suggested that the whole [trial] was a plot by outsiders to help destroy 'the way of life of Southern white people.'" The all-white jury took one hour and eight minutes to find the defendants not guilty.[49]

In a letter to the editor by Sarah White of Memphis, Tennessee, the sentiment was the same. She wrote that "Negros" should remain in the North where such actions are condoned.[50] The identity of the letter writer, however, was in question because four weeks later, Sarah White of Memphis wrote to say that she did not write the original letter dated October 24, 1955, and that her views were just the opposite of the published letter.[51]

On October 10, 1955, *Life* published a photograph of Till's mother, Mamie Bradley, speaking to a crowd in Harlem, New York, and an editorial, "In Memoriam, Emmett Till." The editorial spoke of the brutal murder and said those who condoned it were "in far worse danger than

Emmett Till ever was," which referred to God's wrath.[52] The photograph of Bradley, taken by staff photographer Grey Villet, depicted a crowded scene in front of a supermarket. The well-dressed Bradley, her arm outstretched, was shown in profile view with a stoic expression on her face. In the caption, she described her son's trial as "a sham before God and man."[53]

Her words were proven true a few months later. On January 24, 1956, *Look* magazine, *Life*'s pictorial rival, ran a story by William Bradford Huie about Milam and Bryant. It was a detailed narrative describing how the two men had beaten, tortured, killed, and disposed of Till's body.[54] The two defendants, as well as the law firm that represented them, were paid $4,410 from *Look* for the exclusive rights to the story. In 2006, Gene Roberts and Hank Klibanoff wrote in *The Race Beat* that during the interviews for this story, Huie found out that "Milam and Bryant had not killed Till simply because he had insulted Carolyn Bryant, . . . they had killed him because, in their threatened minds, Till stood for the much larger, more complicated insult to white people."[55] Till's murder would motivate many African Americans into action in the years to come, including Martin Luther King Jr. and Rosa Parks.[56]

1956: SCHOOL INTEGRATION AND BUS BOYCOTTS

In 1956, *Life* published thirty civil rights stories covering 125 pages. Ten of the stories dealt with education and integration, seven were about segregation, four covered transportation, and nine were about entertainment, religion, politics, and other social issues. The increase in stories over the two previous years was partly due to *Life* covering more civil rights events, which happened more frequently than in earlier years, and *Life*'s five-part series on the history of segregation. Through its resources and scope, the series would signify *Life*'s position and opinion with regards to civil rights.

On February 20, 1956, *Life* published "South Worries over Ms. Lucy," which described the three-year legal battle of Autherine Juanita Lucy to be the first African American to attend the University of Alabama. She received notification of acceptance in late January 1956.[57] According to *Life*'s story, trouble had broken out after she started attending classes. Students, who gathered in protest, chanted, "Keep 'Bama white," and "This is plain old war. . . . The Negroes are asking for trouble."[58] After a few incidents of violence, the university trustees banned her from attending classes.

Staff photographer Robert W. Kelly and freelancers Gus Robinson and Don Cravens took the photographs accompanying the story. The majority of the images depicted students milling about or listening to speakers in crowds. One photograph showed Lucy in a bathrobe with a book in hand. The caption stated that she was wearing a new bathrobe that she bought to wear in her college dormitory, but because she was banned from the university, she now was in her brother-in-law's home in Birmingham studying her new textbooks.[59]

One reader agreed with Life's neutrality. University of Alabama student John G. Bookout of Birmingham, Alabama, wrote that although he was not in favor of violence, the riots accomplished their purpose and kept the university "white" for the past 125 years.[60]

The fall of 1956 also was a tenuous time for many schools in the South. In the September 17, 1956, issue, Life ran "The Halting and Fitful Battle for Integration," which described violent incidents in Clinton, Tennessee; Sturgis, Kentucky; Mansfield, Texas; Richmond, Virginia; and Arista, West Virginia. In Clinton, the national guard was called in to bring peace to anti-integration protests, which at times "bordered on anarchy." The article described the situation as a "peace enforced by bayonets of the National Guard."[61] The national guard also was sent to a school in Sturgis, as well as the Texas Rangers to Mansfield. Twenty-nine black-and-white photographs accompanied the eight-page story with thirteen photographers contributing. Four of the photographers were on Life's staff, including Margaret Bourke-White, Robert W. Kelley, Howard Sochurek, and Edward Clark.

The two main photographs on the story's opening spread contrasted in content and demeanor. The largest one depicted a line of eight national guardsmen bearing rifles with bayonets, facing off against a small crowd of at least fourteen white men in front of the Main Street Hardware Company store in Clinton. The young-looking white men in the crowd were standing around nonchalantly, hands on hips with arms crossed. Their defiant expressions contrasted with the determined expressions of the national guardsmen's faces. Although the image showed tension between the guardsmen and the crowd, there was still a significant amount of space between them. The photograph did not show direct confrontation but displayed the anxiety of the men on both sides.[62]

In contrast, the second photograph in the spread depicted three students in profile: two white and one African-American. The caption read, "For the first time a Negro boy sits in a classroom with white students at Clinton, [Tennessee,] High School."[63] All three students were looking down and working, expressionless and intent. Although the African-American student was sitting behind and to the side of the white students, he was part of a class occupying space in close proximity to the other students. All three students were well dressed with short haircuts. Visually, this is an important scene. It normalizes, as well as contrasts, the tension and immediacy of the adjacent photograph.

The most disturbing photograph in the second spread depicted a large automobile driving through the streets of Clinton. The caption read, "Harassing Negroes, a mob, which included women, rocks an out-of-state car passing through Clinton. For four hours the town police stood by helplessly as cars were dented and windows smashed." Older women were seen trying to rock the car. The expressive content of one man, in particular, made the photograph disturbing. In the crowd, people reached out with their hands, touching the sides of the car. One man's grinning expression seemed to suggest his enjoyment as he terrorized the passengers in the automobile. He is looking straight at the camera, which brings the audience into the scene. The contrast with the expression on the two African-American passengers inside the car was powerful.[64]

The other photographs in the spread depicted armed, volunteer deputies lining up for a confrontation, a night skirmish, and guardsmen arresting rioters.

The story ended with six photographs, each showing a school scene of harmonious integration. The first from Elsmere, Kentucky, showed African-American and white first graders standing around tables reciting the Pledge of Allegiance; the second, from Glen Burnie, Maryland, depicted a young African-American girl jumping rope with white girls on a school playground; and another, from Frankfort, Kentucky, showed an African-American football player being congratulated by white fans after scoring a touchdown during the season's opening game. The largest photograph of the spread, taken in Princeton, West Virginia, showed a

Image 3.2.   *Life* published a photograph taken by Robert Kelley of a mob harassing African Americans as they drove through Clinton, Tennessee, in its September 17, 1956, issue. (Photograph courtesy of Getty Images.)

mix of African Americans and white high school students square dancing. The caption stated that thirty "Negroes" were added to the student body without incident. The photograph, taken in a school gym, showed dozens of students of both races holding hands, smiling, and laughing while dancing in circles.[65]

Over the eight pages of the story, the editors at Life led their readers from disturbing, confrontational, emotional, and violent images to serene, playful, and even happy scenes. Because of the scope of photographers and news organizations who contributed to the story, the editors were instrumental in weaving the narrative and outcome of the story. The overall tone was harsh, but the story ended with schools that had found solutions. The headline on the final spread stated, "Without Agitators, Harmonious Changes," and the accompanying text described the peaceful changes that had already begun in some southern schools. Over 185 school districts that year had already been desegregated.[66] By describing violent events in some parts of the country, and ending with more pleasant scenes, Life's story suggested that both races could share the contested space African Americans were fighting for. Although it was still relatively soon after Brown v. Board of Education had been decided, Life had already found solutions to photograph and about which to write.

Another big story in 1956 was the Montgomery Bus Boycott. On March 5, 1956, Life published eleven black-and-white photographs over four pages depicting the events surrounding the arrest of Rosa Parks and Martin Luther King Jr. The two photographers who covered the story were Grey Villet of Life's staff and freelancer Don Cravens.

In early December 1955, Parks, a forty-three-year-old seamstress and youth counselor for the NAACP from Montgomery, Alabama, was arrested for refusing to give up her seat in the front of a city bus for a white rider. In The Civil Rights Movement: A Photographic History, 1954–68, Stephen Kasher wrote that one day after Parks' arrest, 35,000 handbills were mimeographed and distributed throughout the city. The handbills asked for "every Negro to stay off the buses" on the following Monday in protest of Parks' arrest. The boycott was so successful that it continued for more than a year after her arrest, ending in December 1956.[67] The incident drew national attention. The continuing boycott and protests, led by King, were nonviolent on a massive scale. Richard Lentz, in Symbols, the News Magazines, and Martin Luther King, compared him to Gandhi as "not merely [lending] respectability to protest but . . . reawakening the spirit of rebellion in the black church and joining that force to the cult of the Constitution. The great civil rights campaigns would become not simply social movements but crusades."[68] King, along with eighty-nine other boycott leaders, were indicted and arrested for conspiracy, a little known and obscure state law.[69]

The photographs Life published began with an image of Montgomery's African-American leaders with hands raised, voting to continue the boycott. The following image showed a large crowd of African Americans clapping and cheering "the plan for Negroes to show their solidarity by walking, not riding, every place they go."[70] Another image showed the inside of a bus with only two white passengers. Also in the spread was a photograph of Parks being fingerprinted by a police officer after her second arrest, presumably as one of the indicted leaders. A photograph of King was shown next. His expression was stoic as he sat with his hands in his lap and a number placard on his chest.[71]

In almost all of the photographs published with the story, most of them show African Americans and whites in separate and distinct spaces. Photographs of African Americans cheering or walking to work or meeting in secret were laid out adjacent to images of white riders on a bus and an image of Governor Jim Folsom talking to editors.[72] The visual message *Life* presented was that of a separated space.

Also published in the same issue was William Faulkner's "A Letter to the North," in which he, as a prominent southern writer, warned of the dangers of integration.[73] The letter tried to explain the attitudes and reservations of southerners with regard to integration. Although no letters to the editor were published about the Montgomery Bus Boycott, several were run responding to Faulkner's letter. Leslie H. Engram of Cleveland, Ohio, wrote that her ancestors were slaves and she was tired of waiting for change.[74]

During that year, *Life* also produced one of the largest, most extensive packages on civil rights that the magazine ever published. The five-issue series focused on segregation and covered more than seventy-three pages, including *Life*'s first civil rights cover, with a color illustration of a slave auction in Old Charleston, South Carolina. The stories were framed as both moral and social issues, although *Life* described the series as stemming from the "crisis brought about by the school segregation decision of the Supreme Court."[75] Of the 138 photographs and illustrations, Richard B. Stolley recalled: "It was a huge undertaking, and in effect, announced to the South and to America, that *Life* was going to be covering this story in an extraordinarily thorough and active way."[76]

Wendy Kozol criticized the series in her 2001 book chapter, "Gazing at Race in the Pages of *Life*: Picturing Segregation through Theory and History." In it, she examined the complexities of "looking" at the photographs and the many interpretations that could occur.[77] She explained, "These varied ways of seeing were tremendously influential in shaping *Life*'s readers' knowledge about African Americans, race relations, segregation, and the struggle for civil rights during the postwar period."[78] She argued that many of the pictures of southern race relations provided "ambiguous, and often contradictory, messages about race and segregation."[79]

The first installment of the series, "How the Negro Came to Slavery in America," published on September 3, 1956, was referenced by an illustration of a slave auction on the cover. The story discussed the economic and social conditions of slavery, the slave trade, and its political conflicts leading up to the Civil War. Contemporary color photographs of life in West Africa began the essay followed by colorfully painted illustrations of the slave trade, slave ships, and a slave auction. The text explained that slavery was not just an American phenomenon, as the British also owned slaves. This drew blame away from America, framing it as a larger world problem.

One illustration that epitomized the "southern view" of slavery was an 1872 lithograph by Currier and Ives. Its original title, "The Old Plantation Home," depicted "eight blacks of all ages" dancing in front of a small, well-maintained house, pictured as a cottage, with drapes in the front window and vines growing neatly along one of its sides.[80]

A male figure was seated by the front door playing a banjo as four well-dressed children danced in the small yard. Another well-dressed woman could be seen sitting on a log holding a small child. The small yard had a river running next to it, which led to a large white manor house in the background. The color and tone of the illustration suggested a pleasant, happy scene. The caption read: "From this point of view slavery was not an evil but a secure and comfortable way of life for simple-

Image 3.3. *Life* published an 1872 lithograph by Currier and Ives, entitled "The Old Plantation Home," on September 3, 1956. (Image courtesy of the Library of Congress, Prints & Photographs Division, ref. number LC-USZ62-23797.)

minded, childlike darkies, who could live in a snug cabin near the old manse and pass their time happily singing and dancing."[81]

The image presented an idealized point of view of African-American life before the Civil War. Absent from this first installment were images of slave uprisings or lynchings. The next installment in *Life* made up for it. "Freedom to Jim Crow," published on September 10, 1956, briefly described with photographs and text the Civil War, the rise of the Ku Klux Klan, lynchings, and life under Jim Crow laws.

The most disturbing photograph was of a 1919 lynching in Omaha, Nebraska. It showed an African-American man, severely charred and burned lying on top of wood and debris as a large group of white men stood over his body, smiling and jeering at the camera. The men were well dressed, wearing hats, suits, and neckties. In writing about this, Kozol explained that the composition drew readers into the image, "which establishes an intimacy with the subject of the violence.... At the visual level, then, the camera's gaze challenges the white lynchers' gaze."[82] Throughout the photographs and text, the story did not discuss or elaborate on racial violence and lynching, leaving the photograph disconnected as an isolated event. Kozol pointed out that "the layout [and text] disconnects the viewer's gaze from historical responsibility and, instead, aligns it with a national gaze at a localized problem."[83]

The article ended with an explanation of "the lineage of the 'Negro' family" and asked the question "Who, or what, is a U.S. Negro?"[84] The family lineage was centered on the family of the Reverend and Mrs. William J. Faulkner. Some of the portraits of family members were in black-and-white, while others were in color and many of their faces were smiling at the viewer. The text explained the Faulkners were a "typical U.S. Negro" family because most of their ancestors were "white-Negro mixtures" and "only about 15% of U.S. Negroes are of unmixed African descent."[85] By describing a "typical" African-American family and showing family photographs in such a way, *Life* presented the African-American race as already mixed with other races. By framing the story in such a way, *Life* attempted to defuse the argument of mongrelization and miscegenation. The article pointed out that many southern states defined "Negro" as "anyone having as little as one-eighth fraction" of African-American blood. *Life's* story argued that this was, at the very least, an extreme view.[86]

The third installment, "The Voices of the White South," described the lives of five white southern men who were proponents of segregation. They were from different parts of the South with different economic backgrounds: a newspaper reporter and pressman from Louisville, Georgia; a factory worker from Birmingham, Alabama; a mayor from Greenville, South Carolina; a plantation owner from Mississippi; and a sharecropper from Greenville, North Carolina. Twenty-seven of the thirty-six photographs were in color and were taken by staff photographers Margaret Bourke-White, Edward Clark, and Ralph Crane.

The text accompanying the photographs spoke of southerners who were "thoughtful, pious gentlefolk" but were still in favor of segregation. They may have called "the Negro a 'Nigra' or a 'nigger' but have long since ceased meaning any harm or insult by it,"[87] the article explained. In *Life*'s attempt to be fair and objective, Kozol wrote, "the essay gave voice to these segregationists without commentary," and, by portraying them in this manner, "normalized racism as beliefs shared by people from different walks of life" and different economic classes.[88] Through its editorials, *Life* wrote about how racism and segregation were wrong, immoral, and needed to change, but through its photographs promoted many of the stereotypes of segregationists.

The article described Kenneth Cass, the mayor of Greenville, South Carolina, as a quiet, friendly man who helped build a new swimming pool, an elementary school, a roller-skating rink, and a teenage recreation hall for African Americans. The white population of Greenville enthusiastically supported all of these improvements, believing in "equalization" or improving conditions for African Americans but not integration. Even with all of these improvements, the mayor argued "that Negroes [still] comprised the lowest social element in his city," and, the article continued, "the statistics of his police department can be used to support the view." On occasion, the mayor had paid police fines of African Americans who had been arrested.[89] The color photographs accompanying this part of the story portrayed African Americans in stereotypical scenes, and, as Kozol noted, "also [reinforced] the normative whiteness of socially approved behavior."[90]

On one spread, four photographs promoted the ideas of stereotypical African-American scenes. The first image in the spread depicts African Americans dancing to a jukebox. Two well-dressed couples can be seen dancing arm in arm. The only recognizable face smiles broadly as he embraces his partner. The caption stated, "In 'Harlem Café,' Negroes dance to a jukebox. The city operates a more sedate club for Negro teenagers, but juke-joints get more business." The photograph is a good example of a typical night with African Americans enjoying themselves in a "safe" space. The photograph's message becomes muddled when juxtaposed with the other images in the spread.

A second photograph depicted three police officers breaking up a fight between two African Americans outside a bar. The caption read, "Here only fists were involved; frequently guns and knives are used." The caption on the third photograph read, "On the morning after a violent domestic quarrel, a Greenville police judge hears both sides of the story from the sobered participants." The photograph showed two police officers standing between an African-American man and woman in front of the "police judge's" desk. All four subjects were expressionless. The

Image 3.4. *Life* ran a photograph of African Americans dancing in Greenville, South Carolina (originally published in color). The image, taken by Margaret Bourke-White, was part of a five-part series on segregation published on September 17, 1956. (Photograph courtesy of Getty Images.)

fourth and largest photograph in the spread showed the back of a young white girl in the foreground and five African-American men, wearing striped jumpsuits, working in a ditch. The caption read, "Chain gang digs a drainage ditch in suburban Greenville. Negroes may be sentenced to such work for relatively minor offenses. . . . The white girl lives in a nearby house, came out to watch when she saw the gang start work."[91]

Although the photograph was composed in a simple manner, with the girl in the foreground and the men working in the background, the implications of what it represented were many. Kozol explained that the narrative of the entire spread featured images of African-American deviance. She wrote:

> Beginning with a picture of black couples dancing in a juke joint, the narrative proceeds to a street brawl broken up by white police, and a couple being charged with a domestic dispute. . . . The composition [of the final photograph] encourages the viewer to look with the female at the black male criminals . . . the viewer's gaze at the "transgressive behavior" play out common notions about race and sexuality, notably myths about dangerous black men who threatened white women.[92]

Five of the six letters to the editor thought *Life*'s installment was fair and described the men in the story as "Southerners." Mrs. N. E. Cerulli of

Atlanta, Georgia, also voiced a common concern: "No matter how far we of the South are willing to go in 'letting down the bars' of segregation, all of us with children in our families dread the very real possibility of a teenage boy or girl of ours becoming infatuated with a mulatto or colored schoolmate. This possibility forces us to follow our leaders in any policy they name to keep segregation."[93] The concern for intermarriage or "amalgamation" among white southerners was notably prevalent within the story of the five segregationists and within the letters that followed.

In the fourth installment on segregation, Gordon Parks was credited as the photographer and Robert Wallace as the writer. Wallace was given credit for writing the first four installments, including "The Restraints: Open and Hidden." The article, published on September 24, 1956, included twenty-six color photographs, which revolved around Mr. and Mrs. Albert Thornton Sr. of Mobile, Alabama, and their family of nine children and nineteen grandchildren. It described how the restraints of segregation framed and influenced all of their lives. Their occupations ranged from mechanic and farmer to teacher and college professor, and the photographs showed what life was like for African Americans in the rural South. Many of the images were insular to the Thornton family, that is, they described little community interaction: a photograph of Albert Thornton being shaved by his adopted son, as his grandchildren played on the floor; Thornton with his cows and chickens in a field; Thornton walking with his grandchildren down a dirt road; children playing in the mud; and so on. Two exceptions were images of Professor E. J. Thornton, Albert Thornton's eldest son. One photograph showed the professor and his wife chatting with faculty friends at a Tennessee State University lawn party, and another showed the professor in a classroom, discussing anatomy with several students.

Another photograph in the article depicted six of Thornton's grandchildren looking away from the camera through a chain-link fence at a large playground. The photograph and headline above it described the literal divide that African Americans faced each day. The headline stated, "A Separate Way of Life," and the caption began, "Outside looking in," both referring to their detachment from a privileged white society.[94]

Evidence of that detachment could be seen in the story of Allie Lee Causey, one of the Thornton's daughters. She was an elementary school teacher who taught in a "dilapidated, four-room shack" with no water or plumbing facilities. She had recently married Willie Causey, a widower with ten children, five of whom still lived at their home in Shady Grove outside of Mobile.[95] Willie Causey owned forty acres of land, farmed and cut wood for a living, and between his income and his wife's, the two placed the family in "the top financial bracket of the community." Both Causeys believed that "segregation [was] on its way out." Allie Lee Causey was quoted as saying, "Integration is the only way through which Negroes will receive justice. We cannot get it as a separate people. If we can get justice on our jobs, and equal pay, then we'll be able to afford better homes and a good education."[96]

Although her opinion was not divisive and reflected that of many other southern African Americans, it became the catalyst that would change her life. On December 10, 1956, *Life* published "A Sequel to Segregation" by Richard B. Stolley. The article explained how life had dramatically changed for the Causeys after *Life*'s story ran two months before. A disclaimer at the end of the story explained, "In asking the Causeys to illustrate one phase of Negro life in the South, *Life* did not anticipate subsequent developments, nor did the Causeys. In justice to them and our readers the editors felt it was necessary to report further on the story of the Causey family."[97]

The story explained how local residents in Shady Grove and the neighboring town of Silas conspired against the Causeys to force them to move from their home. E. L. "Mike" Dempsey, who sold Willie Causey his truck, repossessed it because of a $301.79 outstanding debt. Rosie McPhearson, who owned two local gas stations in town, refused to sell gas to the Causeys. She said in the article, "People in the North don't understand what we're up against down here. . . . If [Willie] thinks he had restraints before, I'd like to know what he thinks he's got now. It's the burrheads like him that are causing us trouble." Willie C. Allen, the Choctaw County school superintendent, suspended Allie Lee Causey for remarks advocating integration. He was quoted as saying, "We're not used to hearing the word 'integration' mentioned in this county." Earlier that spring, all 102 African-American teachers in the district had been "forbidden to discuss it in their classes."[98]

The Causeys were forced to leave the county and "resettle in a place of [their] own choosing in another part of the South." Writing to her brother about their situation, Allie Lee Causey said, "Here is a mean place [Shady Grove]. The story they did on us is true. The pictures are true. The school is true. The work is true. The home is true. But these people are very, very bad."[99]

In a 2010 interview, writer Richard B. Stolley recalled how bad it was. As he tried to talk to the gas station attendant where Willie Causey was refused gas weeks earlier, it became clear to him "that it was far too dangerous for this family to come back. They were going to get killed." He called the New York office and told his editor how dangerous it had gotten for the Causeys. "They didn't believe that things were that bad and sent [*Life* editor] Hugh Moffett down to take a look."[100]

Moffet, Stolley, and freelance photographer Don Cravens visited the school board, the general store, the gas station, and any other place where they might find the people who were mentioned in the story. Cravens stealthily photographed locals as they were being interviewed by Moffet and Stolley. Some of the pictures were published in *Life*'s story. Stolley said he regretted that *Life* did not let him read the article before it ran. He recalled:

> Had we seen the text on Allie Lee Causey, I'm pretty sure we would have said, "Oh my God! You cannot quote her as saying this." Those were explosive words in Alabama for a black teacher to say, "All we want is equality and justice." And I would have said, "It may sound like clichés to you, but down here, it will be dynamite." . . . I think if we had convinced them to soften her quotes, she would never have gotten into that problem. I don't know that for a fact, but the fact that this black teacher had the temerity to get into *Life* magazine with those remarks was enough to set [the locals] off.[101]

Allie Lee Causey and Willie eventually split up because of the reaction to the story, but *Life* still played a part in their lives, or at least the life of one of their daughters. "Somebody in the *Life* publisher's office was assigned to . . . take care of the Allie Lee Causey situation," Stolley said. Without telling the daughter, Shirley, *Life* anonymously set up a scholarship and paid for her tuition, room, and board at the University of Toledo in Ohio. "Shirley went there sporadically for two or three years, but to the best of our knowledge did not graduate," Stolley recalled.[102]

The fifth and final installment in the segregation series was unlike the first four; it was structured as a roundtable discussion between nine "churchmen," although one woman participated. Evangelist Billy Graham and other leaders of the Christian church debated whether the church should actively participate in integration. By ending the series with a Christian discussion between ministers, *Life* presented the problem of segregation as a moral issue instead of a political or legal matter. The ministers agreed that the Bible did not condone segregation but debated if the church had a moral obligation to help with the integration process. The main conclusion by the ministers was that southern communities were not necessarily against integration but did oppose the immediate enforcement of it.[103]

The outcome of the five articles in the series was to bring attention to the problem of segregation by understanding its complexities, but as Kozol concluded, it also influenced the way that *Life*'s readers shaped their knowledge about African Americans, race relations, segregation, and the struggle for civil rights during the postwar period.[104] Stolley described it as "putting *Life* squarely and uniquely among all other magazines. We announced that this enormous event was about to take place in America, telling readers what the situation was and that they could depend on us" in telling the story.[105]

The segregation series was *Life*'s most extensive project on the civil rights issue both before and after 1956. The first three years of the movement, sparked by the Supreme Court's *Brown v. Board of Education* in 1954 and the lynching of Emmett Till in 1955, brought more civil unrest and division to the United States than in any other time in the twentieth century.

Life's coverage reflected that unrest. The photographs published in the magazine informed outsiders about the South and their segregationist practices as well as promoted a national discourse. The power of the images resonated for those who supported equal rights while creating a deeper divide for those opposed to equal rights.

During the following six years, there would be a steep decline in coverage as civil rights events became more mainstream in the eyes of the media. The events would become more violent and more intense, such as the 1957 integration of Central High School in Little Rock, Arkansas, and its showdown with Governor Orvil Faubus; the Freedom Rides and the bus burnings in 1961; and the riots on the campus of the University of Mississippi. The magazine was there photographing and telling the stories of all those who were involved with the civil rights movement.

NOTES

1. "A Morally Right Decision," *Life*, July 25, 1955, 29–31.
2. George W. Cooper, "Bible facts about Segregation," religious tract cited in Cabell Phillips, "Integration: Battle of Hoxie, Arkansas," *The New York Times Sunday Magazine*, September 25, 1955, 12.
3. Ibid.
4. Ibid.
5. Ibid.
6. Allison Graham, *Framing the South: Hollywood, Television, and Race during the Civil Rights Struggle* (Baltimore: Johns Hopkins University Press, 2001), 6.
7. Ibid.
8. Black Star, a photography agency, was established in the 1930s by three German men (Kurt Safranski, Ernest Mayer, and Kurt Kornfeld) who immigrated to the United States after Adolf Hitler rose to power and created an atmosphere of anti-Semitism and a repressive political climate. The agency was known for its passionate coverage of moral and social issues. See Howard Chapnick, *Truth Needs No Ally: Inside Photojournalism* (Columbia: University of Missouri Press, 1994), 115–116.
9. "A Morally Right Decision," *Life*, July 25, 1955, 29.
10. Ibid. The fourth girl in the photograph was looking down without an expression.
11. "Letters to the Editors," *Life*, August 15, 1955, 18.
12. The handbook, published in 1972, was written as a guide to help those who believed their civil rights had been violated. It contained the policy and procedures of what to do when violations occurred, involving: police brutality, criminal cases, housing, education, employment, voting and registration, boycotts, and direct-action campaigns. This last category encompassed protests and marches. National Association for the Advancement of Colored People, *NAACP Civil Rights Handbook* (New York: National Association for the Advancement of Colored People, 1973), 1.
13. Gillian Rose, *Visual Methodologies: An Introduction to the Interpretation of Visual Materials* (London: Sage, 2001), 33–41.
14. "A Historic Decision for Equality," *Life*, May 31, 1954, 11.
15. Peter B. Levy, *The Civil Rights Movement* (Westport, Connecticut: Greenwood Press, 1998), 8.
16. Ibid.

17. They were Harry Briggs Jr. of Summerton, South Carolina; Ethel Belton of Claymont, Delaware; Dorothy Davis of Prince Edwards County, Virginia; Spottswood Bolling of the District of Colombia; and Linda Brown of Topeka, Kansas.
18. "A Historic Decision for Equality," *Life*, May 31, 1954, 11.
19. Ibid., 12–13.
20. Ibid.
21. Ibid., 11.
22. Ibid., 14.
23. Ibid.
24. Ibid., 15.
25. Ibid., 11.
26. "A Reason for Smiles in 'Back-of-Town,'" *Life*, March 29, 1954, 59–62.
27. "A Head Start on Racial Equality," *Life*, May 31, 1954, 16.
28. "The 'Whys' of Hate," *Life*, October 25, 1954, 28.
29. Edward Steichen, *The Family of Man: The Greatest Photographic Exhibition of All Time—503 Pictures from 68 Countries* (New York: Museum of Modern Art, 1955), 5.
30. Eric J. Sandeen, *Picturing an Exhibition: The Family of Man and 1950s America* (Albuquerque: University of New Mexico Press, 1995), 41.
31. Monique Berlier, "The Family of Man: Readings of an Exhibition," in Bonnie Brennen and Hanno Hardt, eds., *Picturing the Past: Media, History, and Photography* (Urbana: University of Illinois Press, 1999), 216, 218.
32. Ibid., 217.
33. Ibid., 50.
34. "Common Bonds of Man," *Life*, February 14, 1955, 141.
35. Ibid., 140.
36. "One Lynching Spurs Congress to Stop Others," *Life*, April 26, 1937, 26.
37. See "Anti-lynching Bill Is Passed by House after Bitter Talk," *The New York Times*, April 16, 1937, 1; and "Copeland Sees Doom of Anti-lynching Bill," *The New York Times*, August 1, 1937, 2.
38. Berlier, "The Family of Man," 209.
39. Telephone interview, Richard B. Stolley, December 30, 2010.
40. "An Encroaching Menace," *Life*, April 11, 1955, 126–132.
41. "Angry Oratory in Mississippi," *Life*, June 20, 1955, 44.
42. "Letters to the Editors," *Life*, July 11, 1955, 18.
43. Ibid.
44. Paul Hendrickson, *Sons of Mississippi: A Story of Race and Its Legacy* (New York: Alfred A. Knopf, 2003), 5–7.
45. "Homecoming of a Lynch Victim," *Life*, September 12, 1955, 47.
46. "Emmett Till's Day in Court," *Life*, October 3, 1955, 36–38.
47. Ibid.
48. Ibid.
49. Ibid. See also Hendrickson, *Sons of Mississippi*, 9.
50. "Letters to the Editors," *Life*, October 24, 1955, 13.
51. "Letters to the Editors," *Life*, November 28, 1955, 21.
52. "In Memoriam, Emmett Till," *Life*, October 10, 1955, 48.
53. "You Have Cried Enough Tears For Me," *Life*, October 10, 1955, 53.
54. Gene Roberts and Hank Klibanoff, *The Race Beat: The Press, the Civil Rights Struggle, and the Awakening of a Nation* (New York: Knopf, 2006), 104.
55. Ibid.
56. See Hendrickson, *Sons of Mississippi*, 12; and Steven Kasher, *The Civil Rights Movement: A Photographic History, 1954–68* (New York: Abbeville Press, 1996), 11.
57. Roberts and Klibanoff, *The Race Beat*, 128.
58. "South Worries over Miss Lucy," *Life*, February 20, 1956, 28–33.
59. Ibid.
60. "Letters to the Editors," *Life*, March 12, 1956, 15.
61. "The Halting and Fitful Battle for Integration," *Life*, September 17, 1956, 34–41.

62. Ibid.
63. Ibid.
64. Ibid., 36.
65. Ibid., 40–41.
66. Ibid.
67. David J. Garrow, ed., *The Walking City: The Montgomery Bus Boycott, 1955–1956* (Brooklyn, New York: Carlson Publishing Inc., 1989), 188.
68. Richard Lentz, *Symbols, the News Magazines, and Martin Luther King* (Baton Rouge: Louisiana State University Press, 1990), 24.
69. Kasher, *The Civil Rights Movement*, 30–36.
70. "A Bold Boycott Goes On," *Life*, March 5, 1956, 40–43.
71. Ibid.
72. In the photograph of Governor Jim Folsom talking to editors, the caption stated that "Northern Negros sat with whites." Three African-American men can be seen in the photograph. "A Bold Boycott Goes On," *Life*, March 5, 1956, 42.
73. "A Letter to the North," *Life*, March 5, 1946, 51–52.
74. "Letters to the Editors," *Life*, March 26, 1956, 19.
75. "The Background of Segregation," *Life*, September 3, 1956, 43.
76. Telephone interview, Richard B. Stolley, December 30, 2010.
77. Wendy Kozol, "Gazing at Race in the Pages of *Life*: Picturing Segregation through Theory and History," in Erika Lee Doss, ed., *Looking at* Life *Magazine* (Washington, D.C.: Smithsonian Institution Press, 2001), 159–175.
78. Ibid., 173.
79. Ibid., 168.
80. Bryan F. LeBeau, *Currier & Ives: America Imagined* (Washington, D.C.: Smithsonian Institution Press, 2001), 221.
81. Robert Wallace, "How the Negro Came to Slavery in America," *Life*, September 3, 1956, 60.
82. Kozol, "Gazing at Race in the Pages of *Life*," 163.
83. Ibid.
84. Robert Wallace, "The Lineage of a 'Negro' Family," *Life*, September 10, 1956, 106–107.
85. Ibid.
86. Robert Wallace, "Freedom to Jim Crow," *Life*, September 10, 1956, 96–108.
87. Robert Wallace, "The Voices of the White South," *Life*, September 17, 1956, 104–120.
88. Kozol, "Gazing at Race in the Pages of *Life*," 168.
89. Robert Wallace, "The Voices of the White South," *Life*, September 17, 1956, 104–120.
90. Kozol, "Gazing at Race in the Pages of *Life*," 168.
91. Wallace, "The Voices of the White South," 110–111.
92. Kozol, "Gazing at Race in the Pages of *Life*," 169.
93. "Letters to the Editors," *Life*, October 8, 1956, 22.
94. Robert Wallace, "The Restraints: Open and Hidden," *Life*, September 24, 1956, 98–107.
95. Ibid., 102–103.
96. Ibid.
97. Richard B. Stolley, "A Sequel to Segregation," *Life*, December 10, 1956, 77–90.
98. Ibid.
99. Ibid.
100. Telephone interview, Richard B. Stolley, December 30, 2010.
101. Ibid.
102. Ibid.; see also email correspondence, Richard B. Stolley, April 16, 2011.
103. See Billy Graham, "Billy Graham Makes Plea for an End to Intolerance," *Life*, October 1, 1956, 138–151; and "A Roundtable as Debate on Christians' Moral Duty," *Life*, October 1, 1956, 138–162.

104. Kozol, "Gazing at Race in the Pages of *Life*," 173.
105. Telephone interview, Richard B. Stolley, December 30, 2010.

FOUR

The Little Rock Nine, Sit-Ins, and the Freedom Rides: 1957 to 1962

On September 4, 1957, nine African-American students challenged the status quo with the integration of Central High School in Little Rock, Arkansas. This changed the course of history. The "Little Rock Nine," as they became known, were confronted by police, students, local residents, and the state's own governor as they tried to integrate the school. Members of the press also became participants in what was to become one of the most significant events in southern school integration.

Reporter L. Alex Wilson of the African-American newspaper the Memphis *Tri-State Defender* was harassed, kicked, and beaten by protesters in front of the school.[1] *New York Times* reporter Benjamin Fine attempted to comfort Elizabeth Eckford after she was heckled by students and denied entrance into the school by the Arkansas national guard.[2] *Life* magazine photographer Francis Miller was arrested for "inciting a disturbance," or as he put it, "for hitting a guy in the fist with my face."[3] Although Little Rock was not the only city to face trouble integrating its schools in the fall of 1957, it was the most contentious. *Life*'s coverage of the integration of Central High School exceeded *Time* and *Newsweek*'s over the same period. In the six weeks after the Little Rock confrontation, *Life* ran ninety-five photographs on thirty-four pages while *Time* ran twenty-seven photographs on twenty-one pages, and *Newsweek* ran twenty-four photographs on twenty pages.[4]

From 1957 to 1962, civil rights–related stories and photographs in *Life* decreased significantly from previous years before increasing again in 1963. One of the reasons for this trend, as mentioned previously, might have been the decrease in coverage of national news events. Television

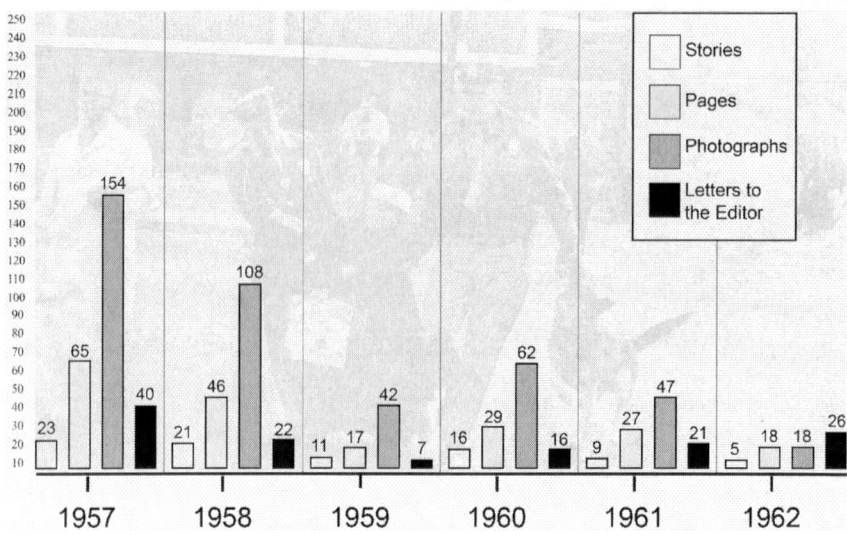

Figure 4.1. Stories, pages, photographs, and letters to the editor published in *Life* magazine from 1957 to 1962. (Created by Michael DiBari Jr.)

also may have been a factor. Former *Life* reporter and editor Richard B. Stolley explained that over those years television coverage increased and became more influential. He recalled, "If television covered it extensively, we would try to look for the thing that television would not get. We would try to find something that would give a different [point of view]."[5]

Television was becoming more influential and competitive each year throughout the decade. According to A. J. Zuilen in *The Life Cycle of Magazines*, television audiences had grown larger throughout the 1950s, dwarfing the circulations of even the largest magazines. By 1957, there were an estimated 35 million U.S. homes with television sets, compared to only 10 million without one. Advertising revenue for television was an estimated 500 million dollars more than that of magazine advertising.[6]

Zuilen attributed *Life*'s decline and eventual demise to several factors. They included managerial and editorial weaknesses, postal rate increases, changing attitudes of readers and advertisers, and the rise of special interest publications.[7] The magazine also lost advertisers specifically to television, "which commanded far greater audiences, when it found itself increasingly unable to compete with television for fast-breaking news events."[8]

Life published eighty-five civil rights–related stories during this period, beginning with twenty-three in 1957 and ending with five in 1962. The articles covered topics similar to those of the previous three years, including school integration, legal issues, politics, and protests. School integration was the most prominent topic during the six-year period. As in the previous chapter, selected photographs and stories in the period were broken down into compositional aspects, including content, color, spatial organization, light, and expressive content.[9] The presentation and framing of each story was examined, as well as how compositional elements within certain photographs related spatially and geographically.

The idea of contested space became more prevalent and relevant as the fight for civil and equal rights increased in intensity. Civil rights leaders realized media coverage and powerful imagery helped bring attention to their cause and sway public opinion.[10] The more southern segregationists held tightly to their beliefs of a southern way of life, the more African-Americans activists became resolute in their cause. As southern segregationists challenged the legalities of integration and African Americans stood up to the white establishment, events and demonstrations turned increasingly violent. Places and spaces where African Americans sought integration became stages for change. This could be seen in the pages of *Life* with the showdown between Arkansas Governor Orval Faubus and the Little Rock Nine in 1957; in the "Freedom Riders" and the residents of Alabama in 1961; and in the riots between federal marshals and protesters at the University of Mississippi in 1962. The contestation within each of these events, which were covered in *Life*, can be discussed in terms of "geographical knowledge," that is, in terms of space and spatial relationships.

In *The Geography of Malcolm X: Black Radicalism and the Remaking of American Space*, James Tyner explained:

> On the one hand, geographical knowledge may be understood as that information purported to explain, describe, and interpret the distributions and characteristics of peoples and places. . . . On the other hand, geographical knowledge may also be understood to encompass a normative dimension in that it prescribes where peoples are to be located. This is consonant, for example, with a more critical understanding of geography, one that takes seriously the claim that social struggles, manifest spatially, are crucial to the structuring and shaping of oppression and exploitation.[11]

In other words, Tyner suggested that civil rights struggles could be discussed in geographical terms and ideas. He wrote that the way we teach children and the policies concerning education were critical to maintaining ideas and beliefs of white supremacy and the status quo. The way our schools taught, influenced, and educated students directly affected knowledge. And according to the writings of philosopher Michel Foucault, "knowledge is inseparable from power."[12] By maintaining the power over the distribution of knowledge, such as in schools, white segregationists were able to maintain their belief systems over less educated African Americans. When this system was forced to change with the

Supreme Court's decision of *Brown v. Board of Education* in 1954, the minority of white segregationists became more desperate and violent.

1957: HARDING HIGH SCHOOL, CHARLOTTE, AND CENTRAL HIGH SCHOOL, LITTLE ROCK

The largest and most significant event of 1957 revolved around the integration of Central High School and the start of the fall term. *Life* also covered the political actions of southern lawmakers, such as gerrymandering districts; the presence of segregation in Chicago; a "prayer pilgrimage for freedom" to Washington, D.C.; and legal cases involving southern segregationists.[13] Central High School, however, received the most attention, most likely due to the confrontation between Governor Faubus, the national guard, and the nine African-American students who attempted to integrate the high school.

On September 16, 1957, *Life* published twenty-five photographs on eight pages along with the first of ten articles and editorials referencing Little Rock, Governor Faubus, and integration in southern schools.[14] The photographs were from Little Rock; Sturgis, Kentucky; Easton, Maryland; Clinton, Tennessee; and Charlotte and Greensboro, North Carolina. By featuring photographs from different places, *Life* framed its coverage as a national issue and not a local event. The first article and photographs reported on how several schools in the South had dealt with integration that year. The opening two-page spread contained four images, two from Charlotte, one from Greensboro, and one from Little Rock; and all four spoke to the direct response of African Americans in breaking the geographic barriers of space in schools. The largest image in the spread depicted five young, white male students in a crowd, laughing and "taunting" in the direction of the viewer. The subject of their taunts was Dorothy Counts, a fifteen-year-old junior at Harding High School in Charlotte and the daughter of a theology professor. In the chaotic scene, the boys pointed and yelled. The caption stated, "Go back to Africa, you burrhead."[15] The jeering expressions on the boys' faces were mean and cruel. The photograph was taken by staff photographer Stan Wayman.

By standing close to Counts, the object of the taunting, the photographer showed the boys in a row facing readers. Also, by running the photograph large on the page, the editors at *Life* emphasized the taunting boys, effectively drawing readers into the scene.

Adjacent to the photograph of the boys was an image of a young, well-dressed Counts sitting placidly in an auditorium. The photograph was also taken by Wayman. A blurred figure was shown gesturing and reacting to her as she pensively looked off the right side of the image. Her expression was unresponsive as all of the students around her watched the scene unfold. The photograph was effective in several ways. First,

The Little Rock Nine, Sit-Ins, and the Freedom Rides: 1957 to 1962   63

Image 4.1.   Stan Wayman's photograph of Dorothy Counts being harassed by a student at Harding High School in Charlotte, North Carolina, was published in *Life* on September 16, 1957. (Photograph courtesy of Getty Images.)

Counts, who was light skinned, well dressed, and attractive, looked similar to the students around her. By telling the story of school integration through one student, such as Counts, *Life* made the argument that there was little difference between African-American and white students. Both races, when sharing the same space, were similar to each other. Second, the blurred figure reacting and gesturing to Counts, was faceless.[16] The movement and a slow shutter speed accounted for this. It also presented the antagonist as a nameless, unrecognizable person, unlike the boys in the previous photograph.

The third photograph in the spread, taken in Greensboro, depicted a white adult male in a plaid shirt yelling at a young African-American boy. The caption identified the man as C. A. Webster, a member of the local White Citizens' Council, and the boy as Jimmy Florence, an eleven-year-old student at Gillespie Park School. It did not elaborate on why Webster was at the school taunting Florence.

The fourth and final photograph in the spread depicted African-American student Elizabeth Eckford walking away from Hazel Bryan, a Central High School student. Eckford was one of the nine African-American students admitted into the all-white high school. Bryan was shown walking behind her, yelling angrily. A national guardsman standing in the background added to the scene's intensity.[17] The story drew national and international attention when Governor Faubus challenged the legitimacy of the federal government by trying to block integration of the school.[18] The iconic photograph was taken by United Press International photographer Johnny Jenkins.

The situation in Little Rock was complicated. Plans for integrating Central High School had been discussed for two years. Daisy Bates, president of the Little Rock chapter of the NAACP and co-owner of the African-American *Arkansas State Press*, helped to organize the nine African-American students and their admittance into the school. On the night of September 3, a day before the photograph was taken of Eckford and Bryan, Bates attempted to telephone the parents of each student to establish a meeting time and place.

Image 4.2. *Life* **magazine published Johnny Jenkins' photograph of Hazel Bryan yelling at Elizabeth Eckford on September 16, 1957. (Photograph courtesy of Getty Images.)**

The students were to be accompanied by white and African-American ministers as they entered the school. Gene Roberts and Hank Klibanoff wrote in *The Race Beat* that Bates was unable to reach the family of Eckford because they did not have a telephone so she arrived by herself and alone. As she crossed the street, someone in the crowd shouted, "They're here! The niggers are coming!"[19] She continued walking toward the school, which was surrounded by national guardsmen. Guardsmen at two entrances around the school turned her away. After being denied entry into the school, she decided to walk back to the bus stop. The jeering crowd followed her along, as well as television, magazine, and newspaper reporters and photographers.[20] In the book *A Life Is More than a Moment: The Desegregation of Little Rock's Central High* by Will Counts, Bryan recounted that she did not feel scared until being turned away by the guardsmen. She recalled:

> I looked down the block and saw a bench at the bus stop. I thought, "If I can only get there, I will be safe." I don't know why the bench seemed a safe place to me, but I started walking toward it. . . . When I finally got there, I don't think I could have gone another step. I sat down, and the mob hollered, "Drag her over to this tree!" Just then a white man sat down beside me, put his arm around me, and patted my shoulder. He raised my chin and said, "Don't let them see you cry."[21]

The "white man" was Benjamin Fine, a reporter for *The New York Times*, and his actions were "completely inappropriate," wrote Roberts and Klibanoff. They wrote he "had inserted himself into a live story—only to remove himself from it when he wrote about the day's events a few hours later."[22]

The main photograph on the following spread depicted eight, well-dressed African-American students being blocked by national guardsmen in front of Central High School. The eight students were the rest of the Little Rock Nine who had received telephone calls from Bates on the night before. The standoff between the guardsmen and the students in the photograph represented the idea of contested space. The students wanted to enter the school to receive an education, and the guardsmen, under orders from Governor Faubus, prevented them.

Also in the spread were photographs of Faubus and President Dwight D. Eisenhower. The former was shown during a press conference, smiling and jovial. The caption under the photograph read, "State Executive Orval Faubus tells reporters he ordered out the troops to prevent bloodshed."[23] The headline on the page stated, "A Governor Flouts Government of U.S." The text that followed explained the "integration program . . . was accepted locally—if grudgingly [but] as it was about to go into effect Governor Orval Faubus ordered national guardsmen out to prevent Negro students from entering Central High School."[24]

In contrast, President Eisenhower was shown descending the steps of Air Force One, looking down and serious. The text stated cryptically, "The governor, however, kept the troops on campus as President Eisenhower hurried to Washington to meet with Justice Department officials. The strategy was not immediately clear but the President had reminded the nation that he was sworn to uphold the Constitution."[25] Also pictured in the spread was another image of Eckford being turned away by national guardsmen and five other photographs of local politicians who were also involved in the decisions made in Little Rock.

The following two spreads in the story addressed the integration of southern schools in Sturgis, Kentucky; Clinton, Tennessee; Easton, Maryland; and Winston-Salem, North Carolina, most of which had few or no problems. The story ended with a full-page photograph taken by Stan Wayman showing Dorothy Counts in Charlotte. She was shown smiling and laughing, surrounded by young, white students. She was the only one smiling. The expression on one student looked more serious, making the photograph seem contrived. The photograph ended the story on a positive note, at least on the surface. All of the students are sharing the same space; visually showing a solution of integration was possible. The editors at *Life* showed a complete story arc with Counts as the heroine. She was stoic and strong in a situation that was difficult and cruel.

Life continued to follow the story in Little Rock throughout the following weeks. On September 23, 1957, the magazine published an editorial on federal versus states rights and an eight-page article on the governor's defiance of federal law.[26] On October 7, *Life* published another editorial on the execution of the law and an eleven-page article with thirty photographs on the continuing violence. The magazine's cover also was about Little Rock, which was the second time that *Life* published a civil rights–related cover since 1954. The image, photographed by freelance photographer John Bryson, featured a compacted and narrowly focused view of Central High as U.S. troops stood with bayonets in formation in the foreground, while white students milled about in front of the school's entrance in the background.[27] The dramatic image placed the troops between the viewer and the school, pushing the events in Little Rock and, more importantly, the issue of integration, into the forefront of the national media.

The text accompanying the story described how the unruly mob in front of the school caused chaos and disorder, fulfilling the governor's prediction about violence occurring in Little Rock. The article stated President Eisenhower ordered "obstructionists to 'cease and desist' from interference with integration." When his order went unheeded, he sent paratroopers of the 101st Airborne Division to intervene.[28] *Life* also devoted two pages to the media's involvement in Little Rock. In trying to compete with other media outlets, specifically television, the magazine provided an insight about their working journalists. Roy Rowan, who was in charge of *Life*'s photographer/reporter teams, reported that after photographer Francis Miller was singled out by agitators,

> a tall, ugly-looking bruiser reared back, cocked his fist and socked Miller flush in the mouth. Miller landed in the grass, knocked out cold. I grabbed hold of the guy who had struck the blow to keep him from going on and kicking Miller. A couple of other guys grabbed me. Then Miller managed to get up and stumble a few feet toward the Little Rock police patrol who hadn't made a move to help him.[29]

Miller was later arrested and taken into custody. Four photographs accompanied the story about the attack. The images, taken by Will Counts of the *Arkansas Democrat*, showed L. Alex Wilson being attacked by the crowd. Wilson, an African-American editor of the *Tri-State Defender*, was dressed in a suit and a tie and refused to run from the rioters. He was punched, kicked, choked, and hit in the head with a brick from behind. Roberts and Klibanoff described how Wilson's refusal to show fear provoked the mob even more. Wilson had been trained as a Marine in World War II, worked as a reporter in Korea, and covered the trial of the Emmett Till lynching, all of which helped him to hold his ground.[30]

The photographs that *Life* published with the Little Rock story were graphic and violent. The first in the series showed the well-dressed Wilson, hat in hand, being grabbed from behind by a middle-aged white man. In the second photograph, a crowd of men in white T-shirts and angry faces watched as Wilson was depicted with a man on his back applying a "stranglehold" to his neck. The caption read, "Go home, you S.O.B. nigger." In the third photograph, Wilson was on the ground, being man-handled by a white agitator. A second man, holding a brick, was about to attack, over Wilson's left shoulder. Head down, hat in his hand, and one knee on the ground, Wilson struggled as the crowd of white men watched. The caption stated that police officers nearby did nothing to protect him or jail his attackers. The fourth photograph showed Wilson struggling to get off the ground as the man with the brick extends his foot into Wilson's chest. The white men in the background continue to watch the action.

The four photographs, taken by *Arkansas Democrat* photographer Will Counts, represented some of *Life*'s most brutal and graphic images of racial violence. They also represented the direct confrontation between white rioters and an African-American journalist, who were fighting for the same space. Although the incident occurred outside of a school, it was an example of how the battle for space had spread to other areas.

The article continued by describing President Eisenhower's decision to send in federal troops, Governor Faubus' reaction, and what life was like for the new students. The final two-page spread of the article depicted the African-American students participating in everyday high school activities, such as lunch, gym class, and a football game. The edi-

Image 4.3. A photograph of L. Alex Wilson being attacked outside of Central High School in Little Rock, Arkansas, was published in *Life* on October 7, 1957. *Arkansas Democrat* photographer Will Counts took the image. (Photograph courtesy of the Archives Photograph Collection, University of Indiana.)

tors of *Life* ended one of the most contentious and violent events of the year on a positive note, similar to the article three weeks prior. The nine students, who were allowed to attend the all-white high school, had been successful in integrating.

While articles involving education were the largest group topic in 1957, *Life* also published stories involving transportation, politics, housing, and segregation in general. The following year was similar with the topics of legal proceedings, education, and political mischief containing the most stories. Of the civil rights–related stories in 1958, nine dealt with the law, six with education, and three with politics.

1958: INTEGRATION AND THE LAW

The integration of Central High School continued to be an important story in 1958. On September 8, *Life* published "Supreme Court Justices

Hurry to a Historic Special Summer Session," which described how the justices were called back to Washington, D.C., to hear arguments concerning school integration in Arkansas. The school board of Little Rock attempted to postpone forced integration for two and a half years, arguing that it "could not operate a public school system under the existing climate in Little Rock."[31] The six-page story opened with images of the justices arriving in Washington, D.C., from their summer holidays and continued with photographs of the Arkansas legislature and other political leaders. The story ended with images from Norfolk, Virginia; Arlington, Virginia; Memphis, Tennessee; and Nashville, Tennessee, and described some of the roadblocks to integration taking place throughout the South.

The final image in the article, a photograph of a sit-in at an Oklahoma City lunchroom, was noteworthy for several reasons. First, the photograph brought attention to another area of civil rights outside of education: a public space in a public restaurant. Secondly, it suggested a branching out of the issues in the fight for equal rights in all facets of life. The full-page photograph taken by freelance photographer Shel Hershorn was photographed above a divider, separating African Americans at tables on the right side of the image and white onlookers on the left. The onlookers watched calmly without reaction as sixteen African-American men and women patiently waited for service that never came.[32] The physical divide within the image separated the two races literally and metaphorically. African Americans occupied space designated for whites only but were unable to be served. The image also addressed the disparity in race relations outside of education. Besides schools, many restaurants and public spaces were still segregated.

On September 22, 1958, *Life* reported on the Supreme Court's unanimous decision not to delay integration in Little Rock. After the court's decision, Governor Faubus and Governor J. Lindsay Almond of Virginia signed bills that closed public schools in their respective states rather than integrate them. The article also reported on one brave, young girl in Van Buren, Arkansas, who stood up against town residents.[33]

Angeline "Angie" Evans, a fifteen-year-old student body president of Van Buren High School, was pictured addressing segregationists during a school board meeting. She announced that after a poll of 160 fellow students, a majority was in favor of admitting African-American students. Referring to the segregationists, she said, "Their arguments are so ridiculous. They've been nothing but troublemakers."[34]

Schools in Arkansas and Virginia remained closed for the rest of the year. *Life* covered the white students' activities, as they tried to remain active and deal with the boredom of the situation. On November 3, 1958, *Life* published "The Lost Class of 1959" and interviewed students from Little Rock and Norfolk.[35] The students' opinions ranged dramatically. "I'd rather go to no school at all than to an integrated one," said Norview

High School cheerleader Diane Milner, and "I don't care if they're pink, yellow or whatever. I just want to go to school," said Maury High School student council member Brenda Lee Smith. The photographs showed students attending night schools and boarding schools, looking for employment, making marriage plans, and milling about "idle and bored."[36] The issue did not resolve itself until the following year.

1959: INTEGRATION AND RABBIT ILLUSTRATIONS

Six of the eleven stories published in 1959 dealt with the school closings in Norfolk and Little Rock. On February 9, *Life* published "Segregationist Surrender," which described how the Supreme Court of Virginia ruled that Governor Almond's order to close nine schools and keep 13,000 students from classes was unconstitutional. Photographs of the dejected governor and politicians were used to illustrate the story. The last photograph in a two-page spread showed seventeen African-American students, with books in hand, smiling. By court order, they were to be admitted into the all-white schools of Norfolk.[37]

On February 16, *Life* published a follow-up story on the students who had integrated into Virginia schools. Staff photographers Paul Schutzer and Edward Clark took all nine photographs. The images showed students of both races laughing and talking to each other comfortably during school. By laying out the story in such a way, *Life*'s editors presented the positive outcomes of integration. Thus, they placed African-American students and white students within the same space in a natural and common school setting. The final image also supported this point of view. The photograph depicted a smiling Betty Jean Reed talking on the phone. The caption read, "Relieved it is over, Betty Jean Reed, in the first week at Granby [High School], calls a boyfriend. Impressed with the casual reception she got, Betty said, 'I think I'm going to like Granby fine.'"[38]

The situation in Little Rock took longer to resolve. On June 8, 1959, *Life* published "Aroused Citizens Strike at Faubus," which featured thirteen photographs by staff photographer Stan Wayman. The story was about how business leaders, housewives, and other concerned citizens of Little Rock voted to remove three diehard segregationists school board members who would not reopen the schools. The photographs accompanying the story were an eclectic mix of images, including people praying, protesters in front of the Arkansas State Capitol building, Governor Faubus, and political groups celebrating.[39] The story, written by Pulitzer Prize–winning editor Harry S. Ashmore, pointed out that the incident resulted in Governor Faubus' "first major political defeat since he called out the national guard troops in September 1957" barring entry to students at Central High School. The governor, Ashmore argued, insisted the real issue was "whether the well-to-do, who live in sections of the city where Negroes are few, would be allowed to force mass integration upon the poor white folks, whose neighborhoods abut areas where Negroes are concentrated."[40]

The governor's idea could be considered a type of "spatial purification." In the book *Geographies of Exclusion: Society and Difference in the West*, author David Sibley argued that "power relations [give] meaning to space . . . and variations in the control and manipulation of different spatial configurations reflect different forms of power relations."[41] Governor Faubus attempted to use his power and influence to create a "purified environment," in which African Americans were powerless to decide policies of everyday life, including education. Ashmore recognized this shift in power, albeit a small one, and concluded that the governor will "never again sit easy on the back of the tiger he has chosen to ride."[42]

Life reported on the opening of Central High School later that summer. On August 24, "Little Rock's Chief Stops the 'Seggies'" was published, explaining how Chief of Police Eugene Smith stood "erect and immovable" in halting about 200 segregationist protesters marching to the school on opening day.[43] The main photograph in the story depicted him standing in the middle of a street, hand outstretched toward a group of marching, flag-waving white men. Behind him stood about eight uniformed police officers with billy clubs. The tension in the photograph could be seen as the first of the marching protesters was about to walk into Smith's outstretched hand. The second photograph in the spread showed the result of the confrontation: a wide shot of water being sprayed from fire hoses across the width of the street, pushing back white protesters onto the sidewalk. The legs of onlookers could be seen under the jet-spray of water. Both photographs, taken by staff photographer Francis Miller, showed contested space, being won by police.

The two accompanying pictures on the following page continued the outcome of the story. The first image was of Calvin Parish, an eighteen-year-old white male, being lead away by police officers. His shirt was ripped at the shoulder and missing a few buttons. The last image in the story showed African-American students Elizabeth Eckford and Jefferson Thomas walking to the high school "under eyes of their white schoolmates."[44] It visually concluded the battle between segregationists and police officers, allowing for peaceful integration. Again, *Life* ended the story with a positive outcome.

Another story of note that year was "Fuss over Integrated Black Bunny." The article described the reaction to a children's book written and drawn by artist Garth Williams, *The Rabbits' Wedding*, which told about a white rabbit marrying a black rabbit. It drew attention from *The Home News*, a segregationist weekly newspaper in Montgomery, Alabama. *The Home News* wrote that the book was "integration propaganda obviously aimed at children in the formative years of 3 to 7."[45] The article described

72   *Chapter 4*

how the book was moved from the open shelves to the reserve shelves in a Montgomery public library. A Florida editor also denounced it as brainwashing: "As soon as you pick up the book and open its pages you realize these rabbits are integrated." Williams responded that he was unaware rabbits were comparable to people. The article ended with a quotation from an unnamed Florida politician: "The book will have to go, I won't have my daughter grow up and marry a rabbit."[46]

1960: SIT-INS AND THE ELECTION

In 1960, *Life* published sixteen civil rights–related stories covering twenty-nine pages. The biggest news events of the year were the sit-ins, which began in Greensboro, North Carolina, and the presidential election. As civil rights leaders and activists increased their efforts for equal rights with intensity and drive, the images describing those events also increased in potency with photographs of arrests and retaliation becoming more common as the year progressed. It had been more than five years since the Supreme Court decision in *Brown v. Board of Education*, and it was the beginning of a new decade.

On February 1, four African-American freshmen from North Carolina Agricultural and Technical College in Greensboro sat down at a lunch counter at a Woolworth's department store and politely ordered coffee and doughnuts.[47] In *The Civil Rights Movement: A Photographic History, 1954–68*, Steven Kasher noted the waitress responded, "I am sorry, we don't serve you here." The boys argued that they should be served because they had spent money at other counters without any problems, and they had the receipts to prove it. A store manager attempted to get them to leave but to no avail. They sat there, unserved, until the store closed that evening. By the following day, thirty students were sitting at the same counter, and the third day brought enough protesters to disrupt downtown commerce. Within two weeks, the sit-ins spread to eight communities in North Carolina and Virginia; and in two more weeks, they had spread to thirty-one communities in seven states. By mid-April, 50,000 to 70,000 protesters were demonstrating all over the South. Kasher wrote, "The explosion of direct-action protests that would be called 'the movement' had been ignited. 'The Sixties' had begun."[48]

Life began its coverage of the sit-in with an unusual photograph. On February 22, it published a dark, almost silhouetted, close-up image of a young man, labeled "a white heckler." In the shadowed photograph, a small rebel flag on a toothpick can be seen through the subject's cigarette. The caption stated, "This man was among the resentful whites who picketed a Greensboro, North Carolina, lunchroom where Negro students have joined a five-state sit-down to protest segregated eating places." The only reference in the accompanying text regarding the sit-in was one sentence: "Raw race prejudice boiled in the South."[49] The photograph, taken by R. R. Russell Jr., was part of the week's news, previously called "A Look at the World's Week." There was no other mention or photograph of the sit-ins until the following week.

On February 29, "Flare-Up over a Sit-Down" described the violent outbreaks during an anti-segregation protest when high school students in Portsmouth, Virginia, clashed with African-American protesters at an unidentified shopping center lunch counter.[50] The first of the four photographs accompanying the one-page story showed a lunch counter where young, white patrons were being served food and drink while their African-American counterparts were not. The African-American patrons looked bored and uninterested but nonetheless determined, while the white patrons talked, ate, and socialized. In the background, two white males could be seen laughing and talking. Although both races occupied the same space in the scene, the African-American patrons were clearly not on equal terms.

Another photograph showed the back of an automobile, which displayed a handmade sign reading, "Stomp out Niggers." The caption read, "Hate sign is driven by white students through the shopping center on the day following the fight." The vague sign did not reference education, integration, or lunch counters, just a general racial slur denouncing all African Americans. The third photograph, described as "angry antagonists . . . glower at each other," showed young white and African-American students confronting each other and about to fight. One white student gripped a small hammer tightly in his hand. The intensity of the scene was evident.

The final photograph showed African-American students "fleeing from the police [at] the threat of arrest." The caption read, "Negro students raced toward the sanctuary of their segregated Norcom High School."[51] Everyone in the photograph, including the police officers, is running away from the viewer and photographer. No faces are identifiable. The compelling image is wrought with symbolism as authority figures chase African Americans across a field.

A week later, on March 7, *Life* published a more disturbing image: two police officers carrying an elderly woman across a street. The caption stated that police officers in Richmond, Virginia, "broke up a demonstration at a segregated lunch counter by arresting 38 Negro college picketers plus Ruth Tinsley, who refused to 'move on.'" The police officers each held one of Mrs. Tinsley's arms as she limply allowed herself to be manhandled. Three photographers stood in the background photographing the scene from behind.[52]

The photographer, Malcolm O. Carpenter, who at the time was a student at Virginia Commonwealth University in Richmond, recalled later that Mrs. Tinsley was a true patriot. He said:

Image 4.4. Photographer Malcolm O. Carpenter photographed Ruth E. Tinsley being carried away by two police officers in Richmond, Virginia. It was published in *Life* on March 7, 1960. (Photograph courtesy of Malcolm O. Carpenter, Library of Congress, Prints & Photographic Division, ref. number LC-USZ62-119523.)

At no time did they "drag" Mrs. Tinsley from the department store. Mrs. Tinsley was a courageous individual who insisted on her rights as an American citizen. Her brave actions that day aided in the tearing down of onerous barriers that had made daily life for African Americans so insulting. The police did not have to drag her, she willingly challenged an unfair system to make her point. To this day, I continue to be in awe of her and her simple, but demonstrative contribution to the Civil Rights movement.[53]

On March 14, *Life* ran a political story about eighteen "filibustering Southerners," who had attempted to stalemate Senate proceedings over civil rights legislation. The seven-page story contained eighteen photographs and one illustration describing the legal proceedings. It ended with an update on the "student 'sit-in' movement" and how African Americans had begun using churches as organizing places. The final photograph in the article, taken by staff photographer Francis Miller, showed a group of five unidentified students in Birmingham, Alabama, praying for the success of the civil rights battle. The image, taken at dusk, showed all five students, their heads bowed in prayer with a sign that read, "Prayer Vigil for 'Freedom.'" The scenic photograph covered a full-page with more than half of the image showing trees and sky. The students in the photograph did not show or emote any type of expressive content as their heads were bowed in prayer.[54]

Although neither the image nor the event was outstanding, it prompted a harsh reaction from one outlet of the local media. On the day after the photograph was taken, the *Birmingham News* printed the names and addresses of the students, which resulted in an attack on one of the students.[55]

Two weeks later, on March 28, *Life* published "For Prayer, Pain," along with the same photograph of the praying students. In a story reminiscent of Emmett Till's, the article explained that several days after the *Birmingham News* printed the students' names and addresses, twenty-year-old Robert Jones and his family were assaulted. The story explained that Robert, his mother, and his sister were seriously injured when eight or nine men came to their home and brutally attacked them with guns and clubs embedded with razor blades.[56]

The second photograph in the article showed a droopy-eyed Jones kneeling in his doorway over "splattered blood" stains. The caption read, "Police made brief investigations, then decided the attack was the work of 'outsiders.'" This time, the attack was not the result of the magazine's published story but of the local newspaper. In December 1956, *Life* had published a follow-up on Willie and Allie Lee Causey, who were forced to relocate after a *Life* story had run a few months earlier.[57] Violence against African Americans, even if it was the fault of the local news media, was still an important issue for the magazine.

On September 12, *Life* published "Racial Fury over Sit-In," which described the violent aftermath of sit-in demonstrations in Jacksonville, Florida.[58] The first photograph in the one-page story showed a street scene of an altercation between an older white man and an African-American male. White onlookers could be seen arriving on the scene. Both men were unidentifiable due to the position of the photographer and the camera angle. The second image depicted a police officer holding a dazed, young, and bloodied African-American male. The caption explained that Charlie Griffin had been rescued by a police officer after being beaten with an axe handle. Griffin, who was described as a bystander, was "pummeled by segregationists" as the angry mob composed of local Georgia residents and farmers "prowled" downtown Jacksonville attacking African Americans. Griffin was depicted with blood splattered across his chest and on his cheeks while white onlookers watched the scene behind him.[59] Freelance photographer Bob Corley took the dramatic images.

The following week on September 19, *Life* published the opinions and comments of the presidential candidates, John F. Kennedy and Richard M. Nixon, followed by an eight-page update and overview of African-American voting rights, leadership, strategy of sit-ins, and continuing efforts at nonviolence. The article described the progress being made by African Americans and how both presidential candidates supported the sit-in demonstrations.[60] The speed of that progress was shown in the opening photograph as numerous African Americans were shown waiting in line.

The photograph, taken by *Life* staff photographer Walter Sanders, depicted more than thirty African Americans lined up against the courthouse in Brownsville, Tennessee, as they waited to register to vote. Three white men casually chat on a bench in the foreground. The caption read, "Negroes—who do not recall a Negro voter in 82 years in the county—wait to register." The text explained that fewer than 400 of the county's 15,000 African Americans were able to register to vote. The process, which was exceedingly slow, went unexplained by white officials. In the adjoining county of Fayette, those few who had been successful in registering were paying the penalty. "They were losing jobs and finding themselves unable to sell anything to or buy anything from their white neighbors."[61]

The space between the three white men, one of whom was described as a deputy sheriff, and the group of African Americans waiting in line was clear and distinct. Everyone in line was well dressed. The men wore dress pants, button-down shirts, and hats, while the women had on dresses or skirts. Most were unsmiling and seemed defiant with arms folded or hands on hips. Nearly everyone in the group looked in the direction of the three white men, the same direction as the photographer and the audience. The effect brought readers directly into the scene. Two of the white men had their backs to the group while talking to the third. The image seems to represent the prevailing attitudes of whites during this time: the space between races was still sizable, but African Americans had the patience to wait and push forward. The article continued to reinforce this idea. It described how sit-ins across the South were successful in desegregating about eighty-five lunch counters. It explained how students were trained to be nonviolent and unresponsive in the face of humiliation and abuse from angry whites.[62]

Although progress was being made with regards to civil rights across the country, there were setbacks. On November 28, *Life* ran a story about mothers in New Orleans "forcefully [leading] children from school in mass exodus that emptied schools of 12,666 pupils."[63] Four African-American first graders had integrated an elementary school in New Orleans and "set off a statewide rampage of hate and hysteria." Representative Wellborn Jack was quoted as saying, "The white man stole this country from the red men and white men are going to be big damn fools and give it to the black man." The two photographs that went with the story were of mothers: the first was a close-up of a mother holding a small child while screaming at a picket line, and the second showed two white mothers "forcefully" pulling their sons away from a school entrance.[64] With regard to space, the photographs represented how white segregationists would rather occupy different space than share it with African Americans.

1961: THE FREEDOM RIDES

By 1961, the quantity of civil rights–event coverage had diminished, but the photographs intensified with each confrontation. The main story *Life* covered that year was the Freedom Rides. In *The Civil Rights Movement: A Photographic History, 1954–68*, Steven Kasher described the Freedom Rides as the "Trojan horse of nonviolent action [where] a select cadre of commandos would be wheeled into the enemy camp in order to open the door to a larger force."[65] The idea was to test state and local segregation ordinances on transportation. On May 4, the Supreme Court passed a decree desegregating inter-state venues, such as bus stations. George Lewis, in *Massive Resistance: The White Response to the Civil Rights Movement*, wrote that the Freedom Riders were "in effect, calculating that certain elements within the segregated South would be unwilling to allow interracial busloads to travel through the region, and would not allow those passengers to make use of the desegregated facilities in bus terminals as they did so."[66] The rides made national news.

On May 26, *Life* published "Bloody Beatings, Burning Bus in the South," a four-page article describing an incident near Anniston, Alabama. The main photograph on the first spread was of a Greyhound bus on the side of a road, engulfed in flames and black smoke. Joseph Postiglione of the *Anniston Star* took the image. The caption read, "Flaming bus, fired by segregationist mob, burns near Anniston, Ala. Twelve riders were hospitalized." The accompanying photograph showed Fisk University student James Zwerg leaning against a building after he was attacked by a mob in Montgomery, Alabama. Wearing a suit and tie, he was bleeding from his nose and his hand. Two buses, which began in Washington, D.C., made it safely through Virginia, the Carolinas, and Georgia before being attacked by mobs in Alabama. The combination of the two photographs represented the results of a brutal attack on the Freedom Riders. The photograph of the burning bus was an example of what happened when segregated space was forcibly occupied.

The following two-page spread recounted correspondent Norman Ritter's description of the violence. Photographer Don Uhrbrock documented the incident. The main photograph in the spread depicted NBC cameraman Maurice Levy on the ground holding his arm up for protection. A blurry figure stands over Levy ready to kick. The blurred effect of the image adds to the intensity of the attacker. Ritter described the scene in a first-person account. He wrote that before photographer Uhrbrock was attacked, he stealthfully took out the roll of film from his camera and placed it into his pocket. His cameras were "smashed to pieces" during the attack, but the film was safe.[67]

The two correspondents were chased and beaten until a bystander found a cab for them. Their incident was similar to Lewis' account. Again, in the book *Massive Resistance*, he explained that when the Trailways bus reached Birmingham on May 14, occupants were met by Klansmen "armed with lead pipes, bats and chains."[68] For about twenty minutes, the white supremacist mob attacked passengers and the media unrestrained and unhindered. It was later learned that the newly re-elected public safety commissioner, Eugene "Bull" Connor, had allowed the mob a twenty-minute period to "have free reign to terrorize those Freedom Riders that had made it to Birmingham" before intervening.[69]

The Freedom Riders were the subject of another *Life* story on June 2. "The Ride For Rights" was a ten-page article that explained how the Freedom Riders were "deliberately and knowingly asking for trouble, and [how] the South was deliberately and mistakenly giving it to them."[70] The main photograph on the opening spread depicted two African-American passengers seated on a bus, as two national guardsmen stood above them with rifles and bayonets. One of the passengers was looking up at a guardsman over his left shoulder. The caption read, "Freedom Rider David Dennis, seated next to Julia Aaron, looks warily at bayonets a Mississippi National Guardsmen has on the bus." The image represented the idea of guarded space that could only be occupied with protection. The passengers were safe as long as the guardsmen were there for protection, but if they were not present, the outcome might have been violence and destruction as in the previous weeks. Coincidentally, the Reverend James Lawson Jr., one of the riders' leaders, "maintained that the Freedom Riders needed no help." He said, "Protection does not deal with the problem of segregation."[71]

When the twenty-seven riders entered a whites-only waiting room at the bus depot in Jackson, Mississippi, they were asked to leave by local police, arrested, found guilty of disobeying an officer, and sent to jail.[72] That summer, more than 300 Freedom Riders were arrested in Mississippi. They were jailed for violating Mississippi segregation laws and were often abused and tortured while incarcerated. By the fall of 1961, they had achieved their goal. In September, the Interstate Commerce Commission issued regulations that successfully desegregated interstate travel facilities throughout the South and the country as a whole.[73]

1962: JAMES MEREDITH AND THE UNIVERSITY OF MISSISSIPPI

In 1962, *Life* published five civil rights–related stories, three of which were about James Meredith's attempt to enroll and attend the University of Mississippi. A former Air Force sergeant, he had received a federal court order for admission into the University of Mississippi, but Governor Ross Barnett had turned him away twice.[74]

The first photograph published on October 5 depicted a standoff that placed Meredith and Chief U.S. Marshal James McShane against Mississippi Lieutenant Governor Paul Johnson. The image ran across a two-page spread with the magazine's table of contents.[75] The image, taken by Flip Schulke, a contract photographer with the agency Black Star, was from a low angle showing the heads and shoulders of the confronting men. Meredith's face was stern and expressionless.

In the following week, on October 12, *Life* published an editorial and a thirteen-page article, "Battlefield: Where the Law Won." Both the editorial and the article were about Meredith's enrollment in the University of Mississippi. The fifteen photographs that accompanied the story included an aerial view of the university, rioters attacking the school, wounded U.S. marshals, Meredith being protected, troops marching in town, and off-duty state and local police officers getting ready for the riot.

By the time the riots were over, 375 people had been injured and two men had died, including a French journalist and a bystander. Governor Barnett, urging Mississippians to "maintain segregation at Ole Miss," fueled the riot.[76] Both John F. Kennedy and Robert F. Kennedy had mistakenly trusted Barnett to maintain civil order in Oxford, which was the home of the University of Mississippi. In the early morning hours of October 1, U.S. troops from Memphis finally arrived on the scene "just as the marshals' supply of tear gas ran out and subdued the crowd." They arrested nearly 100 people, and by 7:30 a.m., after a sixteen-month legal battle, Meredith registered at the university and broke another segregation barrier.[77]

Two influential Black Star photographers covered the event for *Life*: Charles Moore and Flip Schulke. In *Powerful Days: The Civil Rights Photography of Charles Moore*, Michael S. Durham wrote that the admission of Meredith into the University of Mississippi was the turning point in Moore's career. He had been the only photographer inside the administration building, which was bombarded with rocks, guns, and incendiary bombs by angry white segregationists. His exclusive photographs, capturing the drama of the siege, appeared in *Life* in the following week and solidified his "reputation as a news photographer of unusual determination, talent, and daring."[78]

In an altercation with a husky, white, college student, Moore recalled being grabbed and manhandled. He said in *Powerful Days*, "I never took my eyes off his eyes. I have never seen such hate on anyone's face before; it was as if I were vermin. I knew what he was thinking. To him I was worse than 'a nigger,' I was a white nigger ... and worse than that I was a white *Life* magazine nigger."[79] As a former Golden Gloves boxer and an ex-Marine, Moore was able to get out of the situation and remained unharmed throughout the riots. His photographs ran prominently in *Life*'s article. Durham explained that the message conveyed by the article was "loud and clear—and a foreboding of events to come: white Mississippi was willing to shed blood rather than give in to federal pressure to integrate."[80]

One of the most dramatic photographs that *Life* published was Moore's image of off-duty officers gathering before the riots. The caption read:

> The official upholders of law and order in Oxford, a group of Mississippi plain-clothesmen, chortle as one of their number takes practice swings with a billy [club] and another ties on an identifying armband. They are on the campus not to put down riots but to take part in one of the incidents, which led up to it. They mobilized earlier in the week to back up Lieut. Governor Paul Johnson when he turned Meredith and U.S. marshals away from the enrolling office. But when the riot broke out, all local and state cops made themselves scarce.[81]

Moore's photograph, taken over the shoulder of a state trooper, framed the off-duty officers. The image depicted a scene of eight men of various ages, smoking and laughing. The main focus of the image was the man in the center. He is depicted gripping a small bat with both hands, as a cigarette hangs between his teeth. He was identified as Billy Ferrell, an off-duty sheriff from Natchez, Mississippi. Seven of the men in the image were either sheriffs or deputy sheriffs, and all from Mississippi. In the book *Sons of Mississippi: A Story of Race and Its Legacy*, Paul Hendrickson wrote about Moore's photograph. He described them as "sworn keepers of the Mississippi peace" and "leading citizens of their respective communities."[82] He explained that the image had "a lynching narrative, its power tapping into the myth of Emmett Till, straight into all the old nineteenth-century Southern myths of the 'black beast rapist.'"[83]

Hendrickson explained that a lynching must have a common victim guilty of some crime that was threatening to the "virtue or purity of white women"; a community that was totally involved and believed the victim to be guilty; and an outcome of swift justice. Forgoing suppositions and scholarly analyses, he questioned, "isn't each of [the men] requiring the same thing, namely, instant and bloody redress for a per-

(Photograph courtesy of Black Star Photo Agency.)

Image 4.5. Charles Moore's photograph of off-duty officers gathering before the riots at the University of Mississippi was published on October 12, 1962, in *Life* magazine.

ceived wrong?"[84] Meredith attending the University of Mississippi was, in their minds, the perceived wrong.

The violence at the University of Mississippi had been Schulke's first hard-news story involving danger. According to an interview with Jennifer Podis in 2000, Schulke snuck onto campus by hiding in a university professor's car trunk, gaining access to the rioters. Normally, Schulke did not take chances as he had a family, but in this case, he knew "the importance of documenting the injustices" and evils of segregation. He said in the interview, "too many people are being oppressed, and really being oppressed. . . . I felt what they were doing to blacks was horrible, and anything I could do, in any way, to change any part of it, I would. . . . I believe in 'don't get mad, expose it.'"[85]

The intensity, violence, and confrontation in the Meredith story would be indicative of future stories that *Life* magazine would publish in the years to come. The escalation of violence would continue before Congress passed the Civil Rights Act of 1964 and the Voting Rights Act in 1965. In 1963, police dogs and fire hoses would be used against protesters in Montgomery, Alabama; three student volunteers would be murdered in

Meridian, Mississippi; and dozens of peaceful protesters would be beaten on the Edmund Pettus Bridge in Selma, Alabama.

NOTES

1. Gene Roberts and Hank Klibanoff, *The Race Beat: The Press, the Civil Rights Struggle, and the Awakening of a Nation* (New York: Knopf, 2006), p. 177.
2. Ibid., 161.
3. "A Historic Week of Civil Strife," *Life*, October 7, 1957, 39.
4. The author examined issues of *Time* and *Newsweek* magazines on microfilm from September 16, 1957, to October 21, 1957. The issues looked at were September 16, September 23, September 30, October 7, October 14, and October 21 for both *Time* and *Newsweek*.
5. Telephone interview, Richard B. Stolley, December 30, 2010.
6. A. J. Zuilen, *The Life Cycle of Magazines: A Historical Study of the Decline and Fall of the General Interest Mass Audience Magazine in the United States during the Period 1946–1972* (Uithoorn, Netherlands: Graduate Press, 1977), 141, 167. According to Zuilen, the annual volume of advertising dollars for magazines was approximately $750 million.
7. Ibid., 320.
8. See Wendy Kozol, *Life's America: Family and Nation in Postwar Photojournalism* (Philadelphia: Temple University Press, 1994), 185–186; and Philip H. Dogherty, "Varied Factors Lead to Demise of Life," *The New York Times*, December 12, 1972, 7.
9. Gillian Rose, *Visual Methodologies: An Introduction to the Interpretation of Visual Materials* (London: Sage, 2001), 33–41.
10. See Goldberg, *The Power of Photography*, 203–208; Raiford, *Imprisoned in a Luminous Glare*, 4–6; Durham and Moore, *Powerful Days*, 27; and King, *Why We Can't Wait*, 66.
11. James A. Tyner, *The Geography of Malcolm X: Black Radicalism and the Remaking of American Space* (New York: Routledge, 2006), 38–39.
12. Ibid., 42.
13. See "Legislative and Judicial Fronts for Civil Rights: Embattled White South Digs In," *Life*, July 22, 1957, 27–31; "The Negro and the North," *Life*, March 11, 1957, 151–163; "Fervent Faces Amid a Gathering of Pilgrims," *Life*, June 3, 1957, 14–15; and "Vital Verdict in the South," *Life*, August 5, 1957, 32–33.
14. "Troubles Beset School Opening," *Life*, September 16, 1957, 24–31.
15. Ibid.
16. The photographer most likely used a slow shutter speed to obtain this effect. By doing so, the objects or subjects sitting or standing still would be sharp while those in motion would be blurred.
17. Ibid.
18. Jennifer Fuller, "Debating the Present Through the Past: Representations of the Civil Rights Movement in the 1990s," in Renee Christine Romano and Leigh Raiford, eds., *The Civil Rights Movement in American Memory* (Athens: University of Georgia Press, 2006), 173–174.
19. See Roberts and Klibanoff, *The Race Beat*, 159; and Peter B. Levy, *The Civil Rights Movement* (Westport, Connecticut: Greenwood Press, 1998), 11, 108.
20. Roberts and Klibanoff, *The Race Beat*, 160–161.
21. Will Counts, *A Life Is More than a Moment: The Desegregration of Little Rock's Central High* (Bloomington: Indiana University Press, 1999), 34–36. Counts, a photographer for the *Arkansas Democrat*, made a similar photograph to the one published in *Life*.
22. Roberts and Klibanoff, *The Race Beat*, 161.
23. "Troubles Beset School Opening," *Life*, September 16, 1957, 26.

24. Ibid.
25. Ibid., 27.
26. See "The States Rights Issue," *Life*, September 23, 1957, 40; and "Faubus Defiance of Federal Rule," *Life*, September 23, 1957, 28–35.
27. "US Troops Take Over in Arkansas," *Life*, October 7, 1957, cover. A "compacted" or compressed view in a photograph is obtained by using a telephoto lens. This type of lens organizes subjects in such a way, subjects appear to be stacked in front of and behind each other.
28. Ibid. 37–47.
29. Ibid.
30. Roberts and Klibanoff, *The Race Beat*, 177–178.
31. "Supreme Court Justices Hurry to a Historic Special Summer Session," *Life*, September 8, 1958, 24.
32. Ibid., 27.
33. "'Integrate'! the Justices Stand Firm," *Life*, September 22, 1958, 26–27.
34. Ibid.
35. "The Lost Class of 1959," *Life*, November 3, 1958, 21–27.
36. Ibid.
37. "Segregationist Surrender," *Life*, February 9, 1959, 24–25.
38. "Calm and Hopeful Integration Start," *Life*, February 16, 1959, 30–32.
39. "Aroused Citizens Strike at Faubus," *Life*, June 8, 1959, 22–27.
40. Ibid.
41. David Sibley, *Geographies of Exclusion: Society and Difference in the West* (London; New York: Routledge, 1995), 76.
42. Ibid.
43. "Little Rock's Chief Stops the 'Seggies,'" *Life*, August 24, 1959, 40–42.
44. Ibid.
45. "Fuss over Integrated Black Bunny," *Life*, June 1, 1959, 90.
46. Ibid.
47. Pete Daniel, *Lost Revolutions: The South in the 1950s* (Chapel Hill: University of North Carolina Press for Smithsonian National Museum of American History, 2000), 284.
48. Steven Kasher, *The Civil Rights Movement: A Photographic History, 1954–68* (New York: Abbeville Press, 1996), 66–68.
49. "Whale of a Week of News," *Life*, February 22, 1960, 16–17.
50. The photographers listed on the *Life*'s contents page were Joseph T. McClenny, Jim Walker, and Neal V. Clark Jr. but did not specify who took which photograph. "Flare-Up over a Sit-Down," *Life*, February 29, 1960, 32.
51. Ibid.
52. "Lunch Counter Segregation Skirmish," *Life*, March 7, 1960, 42–43.
53. Email correspondence with Malcolm O. Carpenter, July 21, 2016.
54. "The Siege Over Civil Rights," *Life*, March 14, 1960, 21–27.
55. "For Prayer, Pain," *Life*, March 28, 1960, 87.
56. Ibid.
57. Richard B. Stolley, "A Sequel to Segregation," *Life*, December 10, 1956, 77–90.
58. "Racial Fury over Sit-In," *Life*, September 12, 1960, 37.
59. Ibid.
60. "Background for Voting: The Drama of the Issues," *Life*, September 19, 1960, 35.
61. "Claimants of Civil Equality Help Fight Own Battle," *Life*, September 19, 1960, 35–43.
62. Ibid.
63. "'Integration' in the South," *Life*, November 28, 1960, 38.
64. Ibid.
65. Kasher, *The Civil Rights Movement*, 73.
66. George Lewis, *Massive Resistance: The White Response to the Civil Rights Movement* (London: Hodder Arnold, 2006), 137.

67. "Bloody Beatings, Burning Bus in the South," *Life*, May 26, 1961, 22–25.
68. Ibid.
69. Lewis, *Massive Resistance*, 138–139.
70. "The Ride For Rights," *Life*, June 2, 1961, 46–55.
71. Ibid.
72. Ibid.
73. Kasher, *The Civil Rights Movement*, 76.
74. See Lewis, *Massive Resistance*, 146; and "Picture of the Week," *Life*, October 5, 1962, 2–3.
75. "Picture of the Week," *Life*, October 5, 1962, 2–3.
76. Mark Newman, *The Civil Rights Movement* (Edinburgh: Edinburgh University Press, 2004), 84.
77. See Newman, *The Civil Rights Movement*, 84; and Jennifer Podis, "Flip Schulke: A Photojournalist's Advocacy for the Southern Civil Rights Movement" (Master's thesis, University of Michigan, 1988), 17–18.
78. Michael S. Durham and Charles Moore, *Powerful Days: The Civil Rights Photography of Charles Moore* (New York: Stewart, Tabori & Chang, 1991), 14.
79. Ibid., 16.
80. Ibid., 18.
81. "Battlefield: Where the Law Won," *Life*, October 12, 1962, 32–44.
82. Paul Hendrickson, *Sons of Mississippi: A Story of Race and Its Legacy* (New York: Alfred A. Knopf, 2003), 18.
83. Ibid., 161.
84. Ibid., 163.
85. Podis, "Flip Schulke," 18.

FIVE

Fire Hoses, Police Dogs, and the Civil Rights Act: 1963 to 1965

In the summer of 1964, three student civil rights volunteers disappeared while traveling through Neshoba County, Mississippi. They were Andrew Goodman, a twenty-year-old white senior at Queens College in New York; Michael Schwerner, a twenty-four-old white sociologist who ran an African-American community center in Meridian, Mississippi; and James Chaney, a twenty-one-year-old African-American civil rights activist. They had been part of an 800-student group who had volunteered and trained to travel into the Deep South. It was called "Freedom Summer," which was designed to work and volunteer on behalf of "Negro civil rights."[1] On June 21, they inspected the charred remains of the Mount Zion Methodist Church in Longdale, Mississippi, which had been burned to the ground five days earlier by the Ku Klux Klan.[2] The three were arrested for speeding a few hours later by the local police, incarcerated, and released in the middle of the night. Their whereabouts would remain unknown until their remains were discovered five weeks later. Their disappearance became national news. President Lyndon B. Johnson met with the parents of the two white victims. Steven Kasher, in *The Civil Rights Movement: A Photographic History, 1954–68*, wrote that the national media attention involving the case helped end a southern filibuster against the opposed Civil Rights Act and helped ease its passage.[3]

On July 3, 1964, *Life* published a story about the missing volunteers, "The Limpid Shambles of Violence," a five-page article with eight photographs taken by contract photographer Steve Schapiro. The images described the swamp-like scene where the volunteers' burned-out station wagon was found and searchers "hunted for clues." The final photograph of the article showed nine white males lined up along a curb on a street. Most of the young men were smiling and laughing, some were barefoot and wearing T-shirts. The caption read, "While the search goes on, locals—some barefoot—gawk from a nearby bridge. They guffawed when one hooted, 'We throw two or three niggers in every year, to feed the fish.'"[4]

After a forty-four day search by local law officers, FBI agents, and U.S. sailors, the bodies of the missing volunteers were found buried in mud several miles away near Philadelphia, Mississippi.[5] Kasher wrote, "These three civil rights workers—white and black, Northern and Southern, seasoned and virginal—became the best-known martyrs of the movement."[6] This type of violent story became more common on the pages of *Life* in the mid-1960s.

Civil rights–related stories in *Life* increased considerably in 1963, 1964, and 1965 with sixty-six articles, covering the same themes as in earlier years. Although many of the themes were similar, such as integration and politics, many of the photographs of events displayed more violence and confrontation than in previous years. African-American protesters demanded more civil rights in all aspects of everyday life, as racist segregationists became more entrenched and obstinate in their views. *Life's* coverage of these events reflected the frustrations and tensions on both sides.

In 1956, *Life* published more pages and photographs devoted to civil rights stories than in any other year (see Figure 3.1). The most civil rights stories were published in 1964, the highest in the twelve-year study. Thirty-eight stories were published in that year. One of the reasons for this peak in articles was the increase in news events, such as the murders of Goodman, Schwerner, and Chaney; rioting in Harlem; and the passage of the Civil Rights Act in Congress.

As discussed in previous chapters, the conflict or discourses in the fight for civil rights can be explained as a fight for space and the right to determine the use of that space. In *The Right to the City: Social Justice and the Fight for Public Space*, Don Mitchell explained, "Space, place, and location are not just the stage upon which rights are contested, but are actively produced by—and in turn serve to structure—struggles over rights." Many of the sites of conflict were often seen as "symbolic," that is, the actions displayed on those sites consisted of symbolic actions.[7] James Tyner, in *The Geography of Malcolm X: Black Radicalism and the Remaking of American Space*, described this symbolic space as "representational spaces," which were "sites of resistance, and of counter-discourses which have not been grasped by apparatuses of power." Apparatuses of power referred to spaces that were controlled by some authority.[8] These sites of resistance were seen in many of the stories relating to civil rights in *Life* magazine.

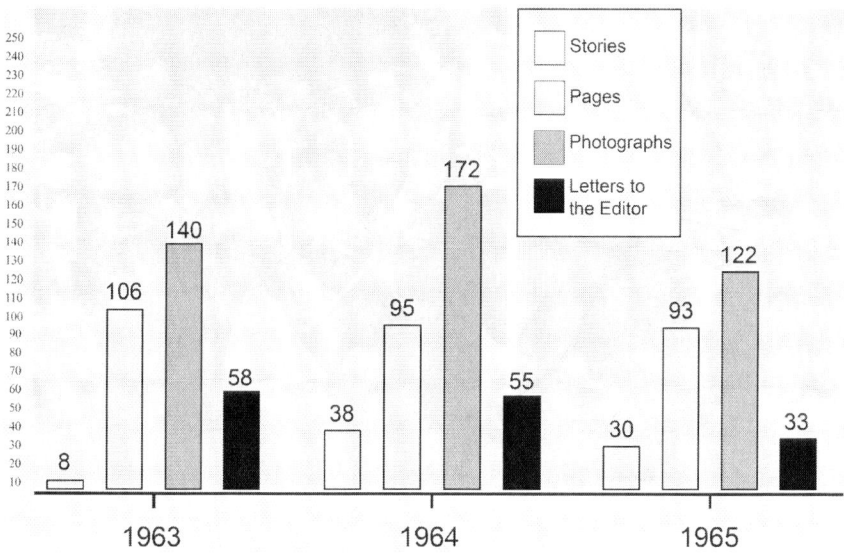

Figure 5.1. Stories, pages, photographs, and letters to the editor published in *Life* magazine from 1963 to 1965. (Created by Michael DiBari Jr.)

1963: BIRMINGHAM, MEDGAR EVERS, AND THE MARCH ON WASHINGTON

Of the twenty-eight articles published in 1963, one-fourth of them dealt with the experience of being African American in America. One example, published on August 16, was "How It Feels to Be Black," a thirteen-page article of memories and photographs by staff photographer Gordon Parks.[9] Another example, published as a two-part series in November, was "Racial Collision in the Big Cities."[10] The two articles covered thirteen pages and featured twelve photographs and thirteen graphs, all related to housing and population growth in U.S. cities. The stories suggested that the African-American population was expected to double in twenty years, creating demands and pressure on all levels of society. As the country faced continuing "moral and constitutional deadlock," the article presented the need for discussion and solutions.[11]

Another quarter of the articles that year were about murder and violence toward African Americans. The remainder of articles dealt with integration, politics, marches, and voting rights. The most noteworthy and substantial civil rights–related articles published in 1963 were the protests in Birmingham, the murder of Medgar Evers, and the March on Washington.

On May 17, *Life* published eleven pages with thirteen photographs taken by Charles Moore on the civil rights protests in Birmingham. In

Powerful Days: The Civil Rights Photography of Charles Moore, Michael S. Durham wrote that New York Senator Jacob Javits credited Moore's Birmingham photographs with "helping to speed passage of the landmark [Civil Rights Act]."[12] Historian Arthur Schlesinger Jr. said, regarding Moore's images, "The photographs of Bull Connor's police dog lunging at the marchers in Birmingham did as much as anything to transform the national mood and make legislation not just necessary, which it had long been, but possible."[13]

The opening photograph covered the entire two-page spread and showed three firefighters leaning forward as they sprayed protesters sitting on a sidewalk. The photograph shows water from the fire hose hitting one of the protesters directly in the back of the head with such force that it created a fan of water spreading out into the street (see Image 1.1). Other protesters were shown huddled together, hands above their heads in protective stances.[14]

The photograph was a symbolic scene, as Mitchell and Tyner both noted, for several reasons. First, the incident took place on a public sidewalk, a place where people were generally allowed to move freely. Mitchell wrote that public spaces, such as streets, parks, squares, and sidewalks, are "gathering places for communicating between citizens and discussing public questions."[15] Second, the jet-spray of water made it difficult to identify any of the protesters as African Americans, and the firefighters also were turned away from the audience. By showing the participants as faceless and nameless, they became stand-ins, or representatives of their people and classes: the white firefighters for the oppressive southerner and the African Americans as the target of abuse. This can be perceived as a battle between good and evil, not between the Birmingham Fire Department and African-American protesters demonstrating for their right to vote.

In "Performing Civic Identity: The Iconic Photograph of the Flag Raising on Iwo Jima," Robert Hariman and John L. Lucaites explained that photographs become iconic when they are "widely recognized, understood to be representations of historically significant events, activate strong emotional response, and are reproduced across a range of media, genres, or topics." They also can shape understanding of specific events and periods, and "influence political action by modeling relationships between civic actors."[16]

Other examples of iconic images were seen in the following spread. The headline, "The Dogs' Attack Is Negroes' Reward," ran three photographs showing police dogs viciously attacking African-American protesters.

The caption stated, "If the Negroes themselves had written the script, they could hardly have asked for greater help for their cause than City Police Commissioner Eugene 'Bull' Connor freely gave. Ordering his

Image 5.1. Charles Moore's photograph of police dogs attacking protesters, published on May 17, 1963, in *Life*, showed passive protesters being attacked by police dogs. (Photograph courtesy of Black Star Photo Agency.)

men to let white spectators come near, he said: 'I want 'em to see the dogs work. Look at those niggers run.'"[17]

As the events in Alabama transpired, Moore's images helped the world gain a clearer understanding of racism in the South. African Americans were unable to occupy the same space as whites, and the streets and sidewalks became their battlefields. Author Leigh Raiford described how powerful and palpable the photographs were: "One can hear the police dogs barking as they attacked protesters and then the sound of nails on pavement and sudden panting as the dogs are yanked back by the chains." She explained that Moore photographed the violence by placing himself in the center of the action. By using short-range and wide-angle lenses, his images demonstrated the "power of photographs for intimacy and closeness, evidence in the photographer's own methods and choice of equipment."[18]

As a native of Alabama, Moore felt a special kinship to the state and its people. Although he did not agree with many of the attitudes of southerners, he did understand them. He wrote in *Powerful Days*, "So I'm there, and I'm watching the dogs being led into the crowds and the high-pressure hoses knocking people down, and it troubled me, because I love the South. And it opened my eyes to the need for change in the state of

Alabama. I saw that we had to become a state for all citizens, that blacks deserved the same kind of chance that I was given."[19]

Not everyone agreed with Moore's sentiment. In a letter to the editor, Don Milton of Birmingham wrote that the editors failed to mention the police officers who had been injured during the rioting and that publishing the article just made the situation worse.[20]

The remaining photographs in the article showed other scenes of the incident, such as wet and disheveled protesters, women being dragged to police vehicles, and an emotional, cheering crowd before another march. The article ended with a photograph of young African Americans pointing and wagging their fingers at a police officer. The smiles and expressions on the youthful subjects seem to taunt and provoke the officer.[21] This image presented a bold and fearless end to the article.

The editors of *Life* began the story by stating how "frightening" and "brutal" the photographs were, and the "Negro strategy of 'nonviolent direct action' invites that very brutality." They described Birmingham as the "South's toughest city" and noted that Martin Luther King had been attempting to force whites to desegregate facilities throughout the city. African-American protesters believed so deeply in their cause that they were willing to face police dogs, fire hoses, or go to jail.[22] By visually presenting the results of these nonviolent, direct actions, and ending the article with such a brazen photograph, *Life* showed African Americans succeeding in what they had set out to do, which was to challenge the authority in Birmingham. Through Moore's photographs, they succeeded in presenting the plight of African Americans to the world.

On June 21, 1963, *Life* published "A Trail of Blood—A Negro Dies," which reported on the assassination of Medgar Evers, a state field worker for the NAACP. Again, *Life* presented the story by pointing out that on the day he was shot, two African-American students had been admitted to the University of Alabama, and President Kennedy "called on the whole nation to help get the Negro real equality." One of the four photographs accompanying the story was of Evers' bloodstained driveway. He was shot in the back from a rifle and had tried to drag himself to his doorstep as his wife and three children watched. He died within the hour. The photograph was taken from above looking down, which distorted the view of the image and gave it a strange, abstract look. The graphic bloodstain was evidence of the brutal and cold-hearted murder.

On June 28, *Life* devoted its cover, an editorial, and a four-page article to Evers' funeral. The cover photograph, taken by staff photographer John Loengard, showed Evers' wife, Myrlie, comforting their son, Van, during the funeral. The opening spread of the section, "Arlington Receives a Murdered Hero," contained two photographs by photographer Flip Schulke. The first was Evers' casket during a full military funeral at Arlington National Cemetery, and the second was a close-up of Myrlie with one tear running down her face. In *Witness to Our Times: My Life as a Photojournalist*, Schulke wrote:

> All people are affected by emotion, and I wanted the nation to see that this family had a father who had been cut down at a very young age. I wanted to show his widow's devastation. I got a picture with just one tear coming down her face. She didn't dissolve into crying, but to me that tear was even more devastating. Those pictures across the casket were the hardest pictures I ever took.[23]

The only photograph on the second spread, taken by Moore, showed African-American men and women running through the middle of a downtown street in Evers' hometown of Jackson, Mississippi. The caption described the anger and rage African Americans felt. It stated that after funeral services, "Negroes screamed 'We want the killer!' The fury was echoed across the U.S. as the Negro revolt gathered force and the potential of violence grew."[24] In most instances, wide angle photographs tend to offer the viewer an overview of the context while telephoto or zoom lens tend to provide the viewer with a tight, more intimate image. In this case, the photograph was taken with a wide angle lens, similar to those from the Birmingham protests, visually placing viewers into the scene. This effect brought intimacy and immediacy to the photograph and story, although at least one person felt *Life* was biased. In a letter to the editor, Randall C. Scarborough of Columbia, South Carolina, wrote that *Life* was more interested in making the South look bad than actually helping the plight of African Americans. Scarborough added that the article also failed to point out any examples of nonviolent integration.[25]

The third civil rights–related story of significance that year was on the March on Washington. On September 6, *Life* devoted its cover and ten pages to the event, including nine photographs in color and nine in black and white. Ten photographers were credited for taking the images, including staff and freelancers.[26] This was an extraordinary amount of resources devoted to one event.[27] The cover image depicted A. Philip Randolph, the organizer of the march, and his assistant, Bayard Rustin, standing in front of the statue of Abraham Lincoln at his memorial. The inside images in the essay ranged from overall crowd shots to general scenes around the National Mall in Washington, D.C. One photograph was of King smiling and waving to the crowd. The caption quoted him: "America has given the Negro people a bad check. It has come back marked 'insufficient funds.'"[28] Overall, the photographs published were not necessarily extraordinary. The photographers covered the event, documenting marchers, celebrities, and politicians who attended the event.

In *The Civil Rights Movement: An Eyewitness History*, Sanford Wexler described the scene as a sweltering hot afternoon, filled with speeches. King gave the closing address, which began as a serious but powerful narration of the African-American struggle for freedom and rights. Singer Mahalia Jackson called out from behind him, "Tell them about your dream!" As King was inspired and encouraged by the marchers, he put aside his prepared text and began speaking from his heart. He said, "I have a dream that one day this nation will rise up and live out the true meaning of its creed. . . . I have a dream that one day on the red hills of Georgia the sons of former slaves and the sons of former slave owners will be able to sit down together at the table of brotherhood."[29]

The march drew an estimated 200,000 to 250,000 people. According to Roberts and Klibanoff, the three major network TV stations, ABC, NBC, and CBS, shared twenty-six pool cameras and set up another twenty-three cameras positioned between the Washington Monument and the Lincoln Memorial. The media coverage was extensive and remarkable. *The New York Times* called it "the greatest assembly for a redress of grievances that this capital has ever seen."[30]

The march accomplished two things for African Americans in their fight for civil rights that summer. First, it was a peaceful demonstration. There was no violence reported. Thousands of demonstrators were good-natured, clapped hands, and sang "freedom songs." Second, as Roberts and Klibanoff noted, the march demonstrated the seriousness and determination of African Americans and their cause for civil rights. King had motivated the crowd with his powerful and emotional speech.[31] There were seven letters to the editors, all of which spoke positively about the march. This was unusual, as in most cases *Life* ran an equal number of letters for and against an event or story.

With such a historic and dramatic event, it also was unusual that the photographs did not have cohesion as a single story or essay. During an interview in 2011, a contract photographer for *Life*, Steve Schapiro, said that because there were so many photographers and about six editors working on the layout in the New York office, a certain point of view was missing. He recounted:

> Each of these editors pulled out their favorite picture, and then would lobby for getting their pictures into the magazine. The result was a long spread, but instead of a single point of view, which has an emotional impact, you had all these pictures from all different people and it didn't have the impact that it would have had if a single photographer had done it. . . . What had been great with *Life*'s stories in the 1940s and 1950s was that they were long stories and usually done by one photographer. And by doing that, there was an emotional flow to the story.[32]

Former *Life* managing editor Maitland Edey explained the photo essay as a "joint affair, always involving two people (photographer and editor) and sometimes as many as seven."[33] The photo essay was also different from any other assignment. "It is not just a group of photographs. It is something more, made from a particular arrangement of certain selected photographs, he wrote.[34]

The violence against African Americans did not end with the march. By the end of September, a bomb had been set in the basement of the African-American Sixteenth Street Baptist Church in Birmingham. Four young girls were killed and one was severely wounded during the explosion.[35] On September 27, *Life* published one photograph of twelve-year-old Sarah Jean Collins in a hospital bed. The graphic photograph, taken by freelancer Frank Dandridge, showed Collins in a hospital bed with white bandages on her eyes.

The text accompanying the image read, "It was a sickening expression of racial hatred, a horrible extension of the irresponsibility of Alabama's Governor George Wallace."[36] In *The Civil Rights Movement*, Peter B. Levy explained that the bombing had "tested the mantle of the civil rights movement and the nation."[37] A speech from Charles Morgan Jr., a white Birmingham lawyer, accompanied the image. In it, Morgan asked the question, "Who is to blame?" And answered, "Each of us. Each citizen who has not consciously attempted to bring about peaceful compliance with the decisions of the Supreme Court. . . . Every person in this community who has in any way contributed to the popularity of hatred is at least as guilty, or more so, as the demented fool who threw the bomb."[38]

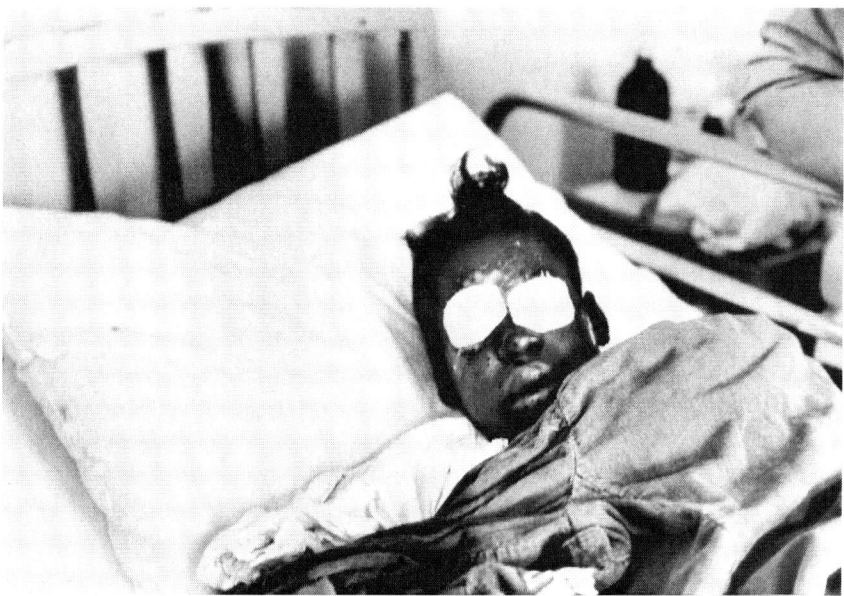

Image 5.2. After a church bombing in Birmingham, Alabama, *Life* published this simple, yet powerful image of twelve-year-old Sarah Jean Collins in her hospital bed on September 27, 1963. Freelance photographer Frank Dandridge took the photograph. (Photograph courtesy of Getty Images.)

More violence would follow that year, with the assassination of President John F. Kennedy in Dallas, Texas, on November 22. He had strong support among African Americans before his death, and according to a Gallup poll, 83 percent approved of the job he was doing. African Americans and their liberal allies mourned his death but also feared Lyndon B. Johnson as president. To their surprise, he proved to be a strong ally with the passage of the Civil Rights Act in the summer of 1964.[39]

1964: THE CIVIL RIGHTS ACT, RIOTS, AND MURDER

The thirty-eight civil rights–related stories in 1964 ranged from violence and murder to education, politics, and fear mongering. The sheer diversity of story themes had expanded to all facets of life. Civil rights leaders such as Malcolm X and King were profiled.[40] Several stories focused on the progress made with the civil rights movement; for example, one photograph and caption ran in May of Linda Brown Smith, who, ten years before, was named in the Supreme Court decision *Brown v Board of Education*. She was now a Topeka, Kansas, mother and "proud to have helped even a little."[41] As tension and frustrations of inadequate political legislation mounted, violence and rioting began to occur more frequently. On April 3, "How It Feels to Be Beat Up by a Rampaging Mob" explained how *Life* correspondent Mike Durham and photographer Charles Moore were attacked by a mob in Jacksonville, Florida. The mayor of Jacksonville ordered a halt to sit-ins there, and when protesters demonstrated against the ban, an African-American woman was shot and killed. The demonstrators went on a rampage, injuring Durham and setting his press car on fire.[42]

On June 19, *Life* published "They Finally Did It: They Busted the Big Filibuster," a six-page article about the Senate passing the civil rights bill. The article contained twenty-three photographs; the majority of them were portraits of the senators who had fought against the bill. The opening spread depicted one image across both pages. In it, Senate Minority Leader Everett Dirksen and Democratic Whip Hubert Humphrey sit in front of ten other senators smiling and cheering after the passage of the historic bill.[43] Peter Levy wrote that the Civil Rights Act of 1964, as it became known, "was the most significant federal legislation of its kind since Reconstruction." The law gave the federal government the power to enforce school integration and gave more protection to civil rights activists. It made it illegal to discriminate against an individual because of race, color, or sex. What it did not do, however, was to ensure the right to vote, but that right would come in the next year.[44]

The following two-page spread showed nineteen images of the senators who filibustered, along with quotations explaining their reasons. Senator Richard Russell of Georgia said, "I reject the idea that federal power may compel the mingling of the races to achieve social equality," and Senator John McClellan of Arkansas said, "Integration carried to its fullest means miscegenation. You can't satisfy them. There is no end to their demands." Many other comments spoke of the unconstitutionality and moral implications of the bill. Alan Ellender, a senator from Louisiana, said, "I am not against the Negro, but you've got to live among them to know them. They're different. Even the Bible shows that. They're not dependable as a race. They're like sheep, you know. They want to intermarry."[45]

Such remarks by southern senators suggested racist and segregationist ideas were still prevalent in the South.

Protests were not just taking place in the South. A ten-page article on rioting in New York City ran on July 31, 1964. The story explained how African-American residents in Harlem and Brooklyn swarmed into the streets after an off-duty police lieutenant shot and killed a fifteen-year-old African-American boy under questionable circumstances. Two of the eighteen photographs were reproduced in color, while the rest were in black-and-white. The images depicted African Americans being beaten by police officers and running through the streets. One image in particular displayed the harsh, violent nature of the rioting. It showed two white police officers clubbing an African-American man on the head while three African Americans watched.

The beaten man's face showed anguish and pain. The photograph clearly displayed an African American as the victim, a stereotype that had been present since the beginning of *Life* in the 1930s. Riots had broken out in other northern cities, such as Rochester, New York, and Jersey City and Patterson, New Jersey. Richard Lentz, in *Symbols, the News Magazines, and Martin Luther King*, wrote that the situation was terrifying and bewildering. Magazines such as *Time* and *Newsweek* wrote about King as a nonviolent prophet who had worked with city officials in trying to quell the violence.[46]

Race riots across the country grew in frequency and intensity. Harlem was one of the first large, northern cities to experience such destruction. A year later, it would be repeated in the Watts neighborhood of Los Angeles. African-American activist Stokely Carmichael wrote in 1966, "Each time the people in those cities saw Martin Luther King get slapped, they became angry; when they saw four little black girls bombed to death, they were angrier; and when nothing happened, they were steaming."[47] The riots grew out of the frustration that African Americans felt from the harsh living conditions throughout the country to the slow and deliberate pace of the civil rights movement.

On December 18, *Life* published "Day of Accusation in Mississippi," which reported on the arrest and legal maneuverings of the men connected with the murders of Goodman, Schwerner, and Chaney. The opening spread, by photographer Bill Reed, showed the defendants of

Image 5.3. Dick De Marisco, of the *New York World Telegraph and Sun*, photographed two police officers beating an African-American man during rioting in Harlem, New York. It was published in *Life* on July 31, 1964. (Photograph courtesy of the Library of Congress, Prints & Photographs Division, ref. number LC-USZ62-136894.)

Neshoba County, Deputy Cecil Price and Sheriff Lawrence Rainey, smiling in the front row of a courtroom. The image was taken during the arraignment of the twenty-one white Mississippians implicated in the murders. Rainey, sitting low in his chair with one foot over his knee, had just placed a big wad of Red Man chewing tobacco in his mouth. The caption read, "'Hey, let's have some Red Man' . . . [as] defendants and spectators laughed."[48]

The image, taken with direct flash in front of the defendants, was symmetrically organized, bringing order to the unusual scene. The smiling faces and jovial attitude reflected in the photograph made light of the fact that these men were participants in arraignment proceedings for the murder of the three individuals. Their actions and attitudes were not unexpected when considering Mississippi's local media. In *The Press and Race: Mississippi Journalists Confront the Movement*, Susan M. Weill wrote, "Mississippi newspaper editorials viewed the civil rights workers with skepticism and even loathing." As an example, she quoted the editor of the *Meridian Star*, James B. Skewes, who wrote, "The civil rights organizations share the blame for the murders, because if a summer project had not been organized, the three young men would have not been murdered."[49]

In *We Are Not Afraid: The Story of Goodman, Schwerner, and Chaney and the Civil Rights Campaign for Mississippi*, Seth Cagan and Philip Dray described the photograph of Rainey in the *Life* article:

> Appearing entirely at ease, bolstered by the warm expressions of support he had received, and confident he would never be convicted, Rainey joked easily with his codefendants Cecil Price, Herman Tucker, and Jimmy Lee Townsend. . . . The image of this crude, smug bully in a police uniform—unrepentant even as he attended his own arraignment on a murder charge—shocked many northern readers and totally confirmed the nation's worst fears about police complicity in the case. Along with his wad of tobacco, Sheriff Rainey appeared to be chewing to bits any lingering illusions about the nature of southern justice.[50]

The text accompanying the *Life* story also reflected the attitudes in Meridian, describing it as "a strange, tight little town." During a preliminary hearing, U.S. Commissioner Esther Carter refused to admit testimony from one of the defendants, who confessed to the FBI, and dismissed all charges against him. The maneuver resulted in a hearing by a grand jury, which succeeded in delaying the procedures. The incident "brought cries from civil rights groups that justice was impossible in Mississippi."[51]

The gruesome story would be a precursor to more violent events in 1965.

1965: SELMA, MORE VIOLENCE, AND MORE MURDER

In January 1965, Martin Luther King won the Nobel Peace Prize. About 1,500 African-American and white guests gathered for the celebration in Atlanta. A few days later, in February, King was jailed in Selma, Alabama, with thousands of others who were protesting voting rights. In that same month, Malcolm X was shot and killed by two assassins while delivering a speech in Manhattan, and in March, African-American protesters were savagely beaten as they attempted to demonstrate for voting rights in Selma. In August, President Lyndon B. Johnson signed the Voting Rights Act into law; and a few days later, rioting broke out in the Watts neighborhood of Los Angeles. The year would continue with a similar pattern: positive steps forward, negative steps back. *Life* published thirty civil rights–related stories that year, covering both the highs and lows.

On February 12, *Life* published "A Remarkable Dinner and . . . Off to Jail," which was indicative of the complexity of events and stories throughout the year. The city of Atlanta celebrated and dined King, Georgia's first Nobel Prize winner. Three of the four photographs taken during the dinner highlighted the hospitality of guests as they ate and chatted together. The largest image in the spread showed King's three oldest children, Martin Luther III, Yolanda, and Dexter, "chattering happily in a sea of white and Negro faces."[52] The photograph was distinct in its construction as well as in its content. The three children were well dressed and seated at a banquet table in front of large plates of food. Yolanda, the eldest of the three, looked up and happily talked to an older, white woman with a camera. African-American and white adults sat at tables talking, eating, and laughing with each other. This was shown as space shared by everyone and dominated by no one, displaying a utopian moment in time. By running the image as the largest one in the spread, the editors brought attention to the idea of shared space as commonplace and normal, a pleasant event that could happen anywhere.

What the article did not contain was that the city of Atlanta and, specifically, its mayor, Ivan Allen Jr., were having difficulty generating guests for the dinner. Gene Roberts and Hank Klibanoff wrote in the *The Race Beat* that Allen met with Coca-Cola Chairman Robert Woodruff in order to persuade local business leaders to attend the banquet and avoid embarrassment for the city. With the fear of the Coca-Cola Company relocating outside of Georgia, "there was a near stampede to buy tickets" for the event honoring King.[53]

The final photograph in the spread showed King leading prospective African-American voters to the Selma courthouse. The caption read, "Minutes later all of them were arrested for parading without a permit. King's arrest ignited the month-long campaign." The article and photographs highlighted the dichotomy of many of the civil rights events of 1965.[54]

On March 5, *Life* published a six-page article and devoted its cover to the murder of Malcolm X and the destruction that followed. The cover depicted a color photograph of New York City's largest Muslim mosque the morning after a devastating fire. The headline stated, "Death of Malcolm X and the Resulting Vengeful Gang War: A Monument to Negro

Upheaval."[55] Malcolm's assassins, members of the Nation of Islam, were later arrested and convicted for his murder.[56]

The opening spread of "The Violent End of the Man Called Malcolm" showed three graphic images of Malcolm X lying on the floor as unidentified bystanders attempted CPR. The largest image, taken moments after the shooting, showed him with his shirt and coat pulled open, revealing a bare, bullet-ridden chest. One woman, kneeling above him, held his head up as a pair of disconnected arms attempted to remove his tie. The three images were similar in drama and intensity and displayed the horror of death in a visually graphic way. The following spread contained a story written by Gordon Parks, which described his final meeting with Malcolm X. He wrote, "Malcolm's years of ranting against the 'white devils' helped create the climate of violence that finally killed him." The last image in the article covered a full page and showed Elijah Mohammed's Harlem mosque in flames. Mohammed was a leader of the Black Muslims, a group Malcolm X had broken away from in the previous year. The mosque had been firebombed in retaliation for Malcolm's death.[57]

Malcolm X spoke of black nationalism and black reconstruction. His message was that nationalism was "designed to encourage our people, the black people, to gain complete control over the politics and politicians of our own people."[58] Tyner explained this idea as regaining control of all political and economic resources; in other words, controlling one's space, both public and private.[59]

Two weeks later, *Life* published one of the most dramatic stories of the year. On March 19, the cover headline read, "Civil Rights Face-Off at Selma: The Savage Season Begins," accompanied by a photograph of African-American demonstrators walking over the Edmund Pettus Bridge in Selma, Alabama. The image, taken by Charles Moore, showed two uniformed Alabama state troopers watching demonstrators as they approached from the bridge.[60]

Selma was the county seat of Dallas County, where 335 African Americans, out of approximately 15,000 people, had managed to register to vote. King, while in jail, wrote, "There are more Negroes in jail with me than there are on the voting rolls."[61] Roberts and Klibanoff explained that King's strategy in Alabama was simple: have nonviolent demonstrators exercise their constitutional rights, causing racists to react violently and resulting in Americans demanding change, intervention, and legislation. King knew that photography and the media played an important role in achieving his goals.[62] In *Why We Can't Wait*, King wrote, "The brutality with which officials would have quelled the black individual became impotent when it could not be pursued with stealth and remain unobserved. It was caught—as a fugitive from a penitentiary is often caught—in gigantic circling spotlights. It was imprisoned in a luminous glare revealing the naked truth to the whole world."[63]

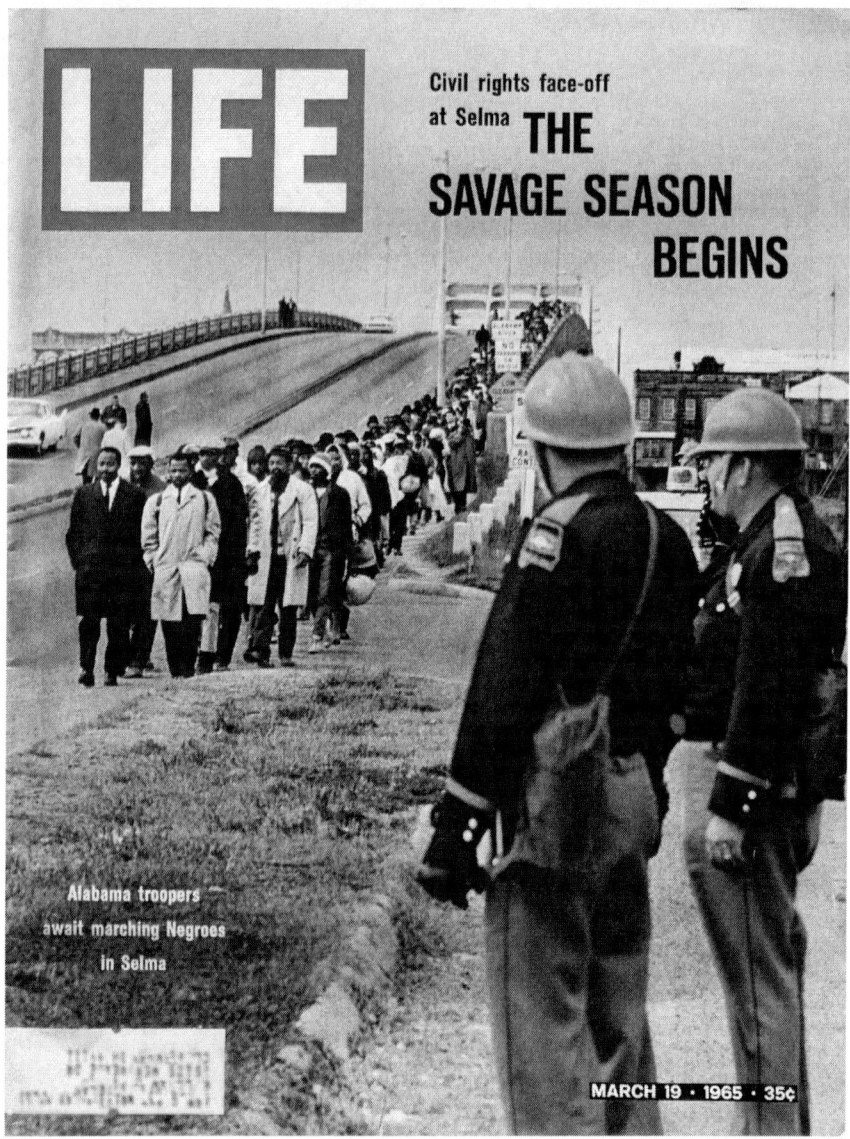

Image 5.4. Charles Moore's photograph of the confrontation between Alabama state troopers and marchers on the Edmund Pettus Bridge was published on the cover of *Life*'s March 19, 1965, issue. (Photograph courtesy of Black Star Photo Agency.)

On Sunday, March 7, about 600 African Americans, led by John Lewis of the Student Nonviolent Coordinating Committee (SNCC) and Hosea Williams of the Southern Christian Leadership Conference (SCLC), left the Brown Chapel African Methodist Episcopal Church in Selma and began a fifty-mile trek to Montgomery. As the group crossed the Edmund Pettus Bridge, they were met by 100 Alabama state troopers. Using his bullhorn, Major John Cloud announced the march to be an "unlawful assembly" and ordered everyone to disperse. The marchers knelt in prayer, but before they were done, the troopers charged with horses, batons, and tear gas.[64] In *The Civil Rights Movement: An Eyewitness History*, Sanford Wexler described a chaotic scene: "The marchers panicked and ran, trying to flee the tear gas, the charging horsemen, the flailing nightsticks and chains and electric cattle prods. Women and children, old and young marchers and even bystanders were savagely attacked by troopers."[65]

The opening spread of "Selma: Beatings Start the Savage Season" displayed three horizontal photographs, the largest running across the width of the spread. The first image showed a row of eight troopers running toward the marchers, some of whom had fallen to the ground. The caption described the scene as "a trooper phalanx [slamming] into the front ranks. As tear gas is fired, the troopers—some in gas masks—start laying about them with their billy clubs, battering Negroes to the ground."[66] The second image, taken moments later, showed the crowd of marchers dispersing as troopers ran past them. The third image in the sequence of the same scene showed a person on the ground with his arms outstretched as troopers with billy clubs walked about.

The second spread in the article contained three photographs under the headline "Man of Peace Leads a Second March That Ends in Prayer." The largest image in the spread showed marchers kneeling in prayer while ominously juxtaposed by the side of a trooper's torso and billy club. A distance between the marchers and the trooper was clearly visible. The divide was symbolic of the racism that was still present in Alabama. A second image in the spread showed a "wall of troopers" blocking the progression of marchers. The caption read, "In a second attempt at a march, a column of 1,500, led now by Dr. Martin Luther King, again faces the troopers who stand shoulder to shoulder on the highway a mile outside Selma."[67] Similar to the previous photograph, the space between the marchers and the troopers was distinct and evident. A third photograph showed King marching in step with the crowd, looking serious and determined.

The third spread contained more photographs of marchers, and another of King as he deliberated strategy behind a closed-door session with other civil rights leaders. The text explained that U.S. Judge Frank M. Johnson of Montgomery issued an order banning the march, forcing a confrontation with authorities. In making the difficult decision to march and risk violence, King said, "I have been agonizing and made my choice. I decided it is better to die on the highway than to make a butchery of my conscience."[68]

The final spread in the article contained three photographs under the headline "Selma's Faces of Defiance—and Death." The largest image was a close-up of an unidentified Selma policeman "ready for trouble." He had a thick helmet and a stub of cigar between his lips. The second image, reproduced slightly smaller next to a column of text, showed Freddy Bennett, an African-American male with a bandaged forehead and a "We Shall Overcome" button on his lapel. Although both images were composed similarly, the layout visually and physically depicted the trooper much larger than Bennett. The scowling expression on the trooper's face contrasted with Bennett's placid and serene expression. A third, much smaller image showed Reverend James Reeb on a stretcher. The caption explained that he had been clubbed from behind by a white man and then taken to a hospital where he died.[69] His death, as Roberts and Klibanoff wrote, "raised the political temperature on an already aroused Washington."[70]

Eight days after the violent confrontation on the bridge, President Johnson personally accompanied the Voting Rights Bill to Congress. He gave a speech that was interrupted forty times by applause. During it, he called for "no delay, no hesitation, no compromise." Then he added, "We shall overcome." Roberts and Klibanoff wrote that when King saw the president on television and heard those words, a tear rolled down his cheek.[71]

Through the national media, the events taking place in Selma focused and crystallized attention on the fight for voting rights in the South. In a letter to the editors of *Life*, Julie G. Saunders wrote that African Americans in Selma had become the embodiment for African Americans across the United States.[72] On March 26, the magazine published images of the president giving his speech along with photographs of the continuing violence in Alabama. The cover image was of King and other clergymen presenting a wreath to the "martyred" Reverend Reeb. The eight-page article also contained a photograph of King watching the president on television.[73]

The march from Selma to Montgomery finally took place on March 21. *Life*'s coverage of the event was published on April 2, 1965. The story, "Freedom March Ends in a Murder," ran on one page with photographs by Steve Schapiro and Charles Moore. The 300 marchers walked for five days protected by 2,000 soldiers. When they reached Montgomery, the story explained, 25,000 supporters joined the marchers at the state capitol. After the rally, Viola Liuzzo, a white civil rights worker from Detroit, was shot and killed on Highway 80 by four members of the Ku Klux Klan. Her photograph ran along Schapiro's photograph of marchers walking with American flags along Highway 80 and Moore's image of a large crowd of marchers in downtown Montgomery. Schapiro's photograph was noteworthy, however, for what it did not capture: the thousands of soldiers protecting the marchers. By not showing authority figures, the photograph visually implied a successful event. The flags, the symbol of America and patriotism, brought the image and march to a national level. No identifying landmarks were within the frame; instead, the photograph showed a lonely stretch of highway with grass, the road, the marchers, and trees in the background. The space was nondescript.[74] The road might have been in Ohio, Illinois, or Vermont. The photograph became a symbol of success for all Americans.

President Johnson signed the Voting Rights Act into law on August 6, 1965. Roberts and Klibanoff wrote, "It was arguably the most remarkable victory of the entire civil rights era. . . . This was the high point."[75] On August 20, *Life* published "The New Voting Law Goes into Action," a two-page spread containing three images. The first image, covering a full page, showed President Johnson signing the bill into law in the President's Room of the White House. The caption read, "In this room 104 years before, Abraham Lincoln signed a bill freeing the slaves." Behind the president was a group of senators and congressmen. A second photo, on the adjoining page, showed a seated African-American woman, a baby in her arms, and an extravagant hat on her head, waiting to register to vote at a post office in Demopolis, Alabama. A line of people behind can be seen patiently waiting to register. She was shown intently staring off to the left, which led the viewer to the photograph of Johnson. The third photograph in the spread showed Charlie Jones, an eighty-seven-year-old resident of Greensboro, Alabama, filling out registration forms. The text explained how U.S. registrars "inscribed the names of 1,144 Negroes who had heeded the President's plea: 'You must vote . . . the vote is the most powerful instrument ever devised by man for breaking down injustice.'"[76]

The design and photographs of the article compared two very different worlds: the president with his entourage in a beautiful, ornate room, while African Americans waited to register to vote in a post office with fluorescent lights and pipes hanging from the ceiling. The images could not have been more dissimilar, both visually and thematically. The president spoke of breaking down the walls of injustice, but the images reflected the opposite, visually describing the gap between the wealthy and the poor.

Violence and dissatisfaction would continue when, five days after the signing of the bill, rioting broke out in the Watts neighborhood of Los Angeles. Kasher described the uprising as "the most violent racial rebellion in U.S. history." Fourteen thousand national guardsmen were sent to control the looting and rioting. Four thousand people were jailed; thirty-four people were killed, and one thousand were injured.[77] On August 7, *Life* published fifteen pages and devoted its cover to the violence and destruction in Los Angeles. The images and tone of the photographs had changed. African Americans were no longer portrayed as victims. Their expressions had become meaner, harder. They were shown throwing rocks, stealing items off shelves, and running down the street with armfuls of merchandise. They had guns. They yelled slurs like "Get Whitey!" and "Burn, baby, burn" as the destruction raged throughout the city.[78]

Levy wrote that the rage African Americans felt grew from a society "pervaded by racial, social, and economic inequality. The riots also revealed the shortcomings of the mainstream civil rights movement, which until Watts was focused primarily on the problems of southern blacks."[79] The civil rights movement changed direction after the riots, becoming more violent and confrontational.

King told reporters that Watts was "a class revolt of underprivileged against the privileged" and pleaded with the mayor, the police chief, and governor to do something about the underlying causes of the rioting, but they angrily dismissed him. Later, he would say, "The decade of 1955 to 1965, with its constructive elements, misled us. Everyone underestimated the amount of rage Negroes were suppressing, and the amount of bigotry in the white majority was disgusting."

NOTES

1. "The Limpid Shambles of Violence," *Life*, July 3, 1964, 32–34b.
2. Seth Cagin and Philip Dray, *We Are Not Afraid: The Story of Goodman, Schwerner and Chaney and the Civil Rights Campaign for Mississippi* (New York: Macmillan Publishing, 1988), 1.
3. Steven Kasher, *The Civil Rights Movement: A Photographic History, 1954–68* (New York: Abbeville Press, 1996), 140.
4. "The Limpid Shambles of Violence," 32–34b.
5. Gene Roberts and Hank Klibanoff, *The Race Beat: The Press, the Civil Rights Struggle, and the Awakening of a Nation* (New York: Knopf, 2006), 364.
6. Kasher, *The Civil Rights Movement*, 140.
7. Don Mitchell, *The Right to the City: Social Justice and the Fight for Public Space* (New York: Guilford Press, 2003), 81–82.
8. James A. Tyner, *The Geography of Malcolm X: Black Radicalism and the Remaking of American Space* (New York: Routledge, 2006), 63–64.
9. "How It Feels to Be Black," *Life*, August 16, 1963, 72–83.
10. See Theodore H. White, "Racial Collision in the Big Cities," *Life*, November 2, 1963, 100–120; and Theodore H. White, "Power Structure, Integration, Militancy, Freedom Now!" *Life*, November 29, 1963, 78–93.
11. Ibid.
12. Michael S. Durham and Charles Moore, *Powerful Days: The Civil Rights Photography of Charles Moore* (New York: Stewart, Tabori & Chang, 1991), 32.
13. White, "Racial Collision in the Big Cities," 100–120.
14. "They Fight a Fire That Won't Go Out," *Life*, May 17, 1963, 28–36.
15. Mitchell, *The Right to the City*, 130.
16. Robert Hariman and John L. Lucaites, "Performing Civic Identity: The Iconic Photograph of the Flag Raising on Iwo Jima," *Quarterly Journal of Speech* 88 (November 2002), 366.
17. "They Fight a Fire That Won't Go Out," 30–31.
18. Leigh Raiford, *Imprisoned in a Luminous Glare: Photography and the African American Freedom Struggle* (Chapel Hill: University of North Carolina Press, 2011), 81–82.
19. Durham and Moore, *Powerful Days*, 32–33.

20. Ibid.
21. "They Fight a Fire That Won't Go Out," 32–36.
22. Ibid.
23. Flip Schulke with Matt Schudel, *Witness to Our Times: My Life as a Photojournalist* (Chicago: Carus Publishing, 2003), 30.
24. Myrlie Evers, "Arlington Receives a Murdered Hero," *Life*, June 28, 1963, 34–37.
25. "Letters to the Editors," *Life*, July 19, 1963, 21.
26. The photographers listed were: Paul Schutzer, Gordon Parks, Francis Miller, and Elliott Elisofon, and freelancers Gordon Tenney, Jim Maman, Frank Dandridge, Steve Schapiro, Bob Gomel, and Charles Moore.
27. *Life* using ten photographers to cover one event was an unusually high number. For the presidential inauguration of John F. Kennedy in January of 1961, *Life* used six photographers, and for the presidential inauguration of Lyndon B. Johnson in January of 1965, *Life* used eight photographers. Both were large, planned events in Washington, D.C.
28. "They Come Marching Up Conscience Road," *Life*, September 6, 1963, 20–29.
29. Sanford Wexler, *The Civil Rights Movement: An Eyewitness History* (New York: Facts on File, 1993), 182.
30. Roberts and Klibanoff, *The Race Beat*, 346.
31. Ibid., 349.
32. Telephone interview, Steve Schapiro, February 8, 2011.
33. Maitland Edey, *Great Photographic Essays from* Life (Boston: New York Graphic Society, Little, Brown and Company, 1978), 5.
34. Ibid., 6.
35. *Life* reported that three girls had been killed in the bombing, although later accounts reported four young girls had died and nearly twenty others wounded. See Charles Morgan Jr., "Birmingham: An Alabaman's Great Speech Lays the Blame," September 27, 1963, 44b–44c; and Peter B. Levy, *The Civil Rights Movement* (New York: Greenwood Press, 1998), 23.
36. Morgan, "Birmingham," 44b–44c.
37. Levy, *The Civil Rights Movement*, 23.
38. Morgan, "Birmingham," 44b–44c.
39. Levy, *The Civil Rights Movement*, 24.
40. See Marc Crawford, "The Ominous Malcolm X Exits from the Muslims," *Life*, March 20, 1964, 40–40a; and Martin Luther King Jr., "Why We Can't Wait," *Life*, May 15, 1964, 98–106.
41. "Segregation's Celebrity 10 Years Later," *Life*, May 22, 1964, 46d.
42. See "How It Feels to Be Beat Up by a Rampaging Mob," *Life*, April 3, 1964, 44–45; "Maryland, My Maryland, the Bayonets and the Cameras Flash," *Life*, May 22, 1964, 46c; and "Harlem's 'Long Hot Summer' Begins," *Life*, July 31, 1964, 14–23.
43. "They Finally Did It: They Busted the Big Filibuster," *Life*, June 19, 1964, 32–37.
44. Levy, *The Civil Rights Movement*, 24.
45. "They Finally Did It," 32–37.
46. Richard Lentz, *Symbols, the News Magazines, and Martin Luther King* (Baton Rouge: Louisiana State University Press, 1990), 129–131.
47. Levy, *The Civil Rights Movement*, 189.
48. "Day of Accusation in Mississippi," *Life*, December 18, 1964, 34–39.
49. Susan M. Weill, "Mississippi's Daily Press in Three Crises," in David R. Davies, *The Press and Race: Mississippi Journalists Confront the Movement* (Jackson: University Press of Mississippi, 2001), 41, 43.
50. Cagin and Dray, *We Are Not Afraid*, 378.
51. "Day of Accusation in Mississippi," 34–39.
52. "A Remarkable Dinner and . . . Off to Jail," *Life*, February 12, 1965, 34–34a.
53. Roberts and Klibanoff, *The Race Beat*, 381–382.
54. Ibid.

55. "Death of Malcolm X and the Resulting Vengeful Gang War: A Monument to Negro Upheaval." *Life*, March 5, 1965, cover.
56. Levy, *The Civil Rights Movement*, 137.
57. "The Violent End of the Man Called Malcolm," *Life*, March 5, 1965, 26–31.
58. Levy, *The Civil Rights Movement*, 185.
59. Tyner, *The Geography of Malcolm X*, 99.
60. "Selma: Beatings Start the Savage Season," *Life*, March 19, cover.
61. Roberts and Klibanoff, *The Race Beat*, 375–376, 382.
62. Ibid.
63. Martin Luther King Jr., *Why We Can't Wait* (New York: New American Library, 1964), 39.
64. Roberts and Klibanoff, *The Race Beat*, 385.
65. Wexler, *The Civil Rights Movement*, 220.
66. "Selma: Beatings Start the Savage Season," 30–37.
67. Ibid.
68. Ibid.
69. Ibid.
70. Roberts and Klibanoff, *The Race Beat*, 388.
71. Ibid.
72. "Letters to the Editors," *Life*, April 9, 1965, 18.
73. "The Nation Surges to Join the Negro on His March," *Life*, March 26, 1965, cover, 30–37.
74. "Freedom March Ends in a Murder," *Life*, April 2, 1965, 45.
75. Roberts and Klibanoff, *The Race Beat*, 394.
76. "The New Voting Law Goes into Action," *Life*, August 20, 1965, 34–34a.
77. Kasher, *The Civil Rights Movement*, 216.
78. "Out of a Cauldron of Hate—Arson and Death," *Life*, August 27, 1965, 20–34.
79. Levy, *The Civil Rights Movement*, 29.

SIX

Life Magazine and the Civil Rights Movement

On Sunday morning, September 15, 1964, a bomb exploded at the Sixteenth Street Baptist Church in Birmingham. Blocks away, rock and glass debris could be seen flying through the air. The church was celebrating Youth Day when the bomb exploded. Four young girls, ages eleven to fourteen, were killed, and twenty-one children were injured.[1] Days later, reporter Hal Wingo found himself in the layout room at *Life*'s offices in New York City looking at photographs from the bombing with Managing Editor George Hunt. They spread the photographs on the floor and walked around them, stopping whenever one caught their eye. Wingo recalled that Hunt kept stopping and looking at one image of a young girl in a hospital bed with patches over her eyes (see Image 5.2). "You could tell he was moved by it," Wingo said. Finally, Hunt picked the picture up and said, "This is the one." The photograph got to the strength of what *Life* magazine could do at a time of such horrific unrest and tension in the country. "You couldn't just walk away [from it]; you couldn't turn off the television screen; you couldn't avoid looking at the picture . . . and seeing what it represented. Even people who hated *Life* would have looked at it, and somewhere deep down in themselves say, 'We bear some responsibility in this,'" Wingo recalled during an interview.[2]

By publishing such dramatic and poignant photographs, *Life* magazine pushed the inequities of racism into the American discourse. Along with the leaders of the civil rights movement, the power and influence of such a popular and visual periodical affected change. Whether on purpose or by happenstance, *Life* helped the world to see the reality of men's harsh actions.

Civil rights leaders such as Martin Luther King knew the power of photography and the media. King knew that if the cameras caught the violence and blood and snarling dogs, the world would be the witness. When he told photographer Flip Schulke that he should not have gotten involved when African-American children had been pushed to the ground in March 1965, he knew that moment had not been documented. He told Schulke, "What is important is for you to do what you're supposed to do, and that is to record and communicate to the rest of the world what's going on here. You have to stay back, and not listen to your gut. You've got to do what you were sent here to do, and that is to keep the camera shooting."[3] Leigh Raiford wrote that the images from the civil rights era "challenged an entire economic and social regime of power." And the photograph "proved a tool as effective as bus boycotts and as righteous as nonviolence."[4] Photography helped to change people's perceptions and attitudes. Photographs of violence abuse, death, murder, and an injured child who was blinded by a bomb contributed to the change toward equal rights.

Life magazine became the catalyst of that change and a vehicle for Schulke and many other photographers during the civil rights debate. It began with Luce's 1936 prospectus, which launched the magazine and set the stage for its extraordinary run of thirty-six years as a leader, not just in the nation's changing media landscape, but in how generations viewed their world. It explained the magazine's purpose: "To see life; to see the world; to eyewitness great events . . . to see and be amazed; to see and be instructed."[5] In Life's *America: Family and Nation in Postwar Photojournalism*, Wendy Kozol wrote that this statement "revealed a belief, and also a conceit, that the camera, and therefore *Life*, has the power to reveal the world." She explained that "seeing" became not a mirror "but a way of framing differences and forming boundaries to define normative society."[6]

After the Supreme Court's *Brown v. Board of Education* decision in 1954, the editors at *Life* decided the magazine would play a more proactive role in covering integration in public schools, more so than *Time* or *Look*. Former Atlanta bureau editor Richard B. Stolley recalled that the magazine's five-part series on segregation, published in September and October 1956, "was a huge undertaking, and, in effect, announced to the South and to America that *Life* was going to be covering this story in an extraordinary thorough and active way."[7]

In many ways, *Life* did cover civil rights as no other news magazine or organization before or since, but it was not that simple. From 1954 to 1965, it published 227 civil rights–related articles and 1,200 photographs, an average of almost nineteen stories and 100 photographs per year. The amount of resources and energy the magazine allocated to the civil rights movement and school integration was enormous. An example was the 1957 integration of Central High School in Little Rock, Arkansas. Over a six-week time period, *Life*'s coverage of the story exceeded *Time* and *Newsweek*'s in photographs and pages.[8] Throughout this study of twelve years of *Life*'s coverage, the magazine devoted resources to every major civil rights event.

Life magazine editors and photographers believed that they could affect people and create change. Stolley said that it did this in two ways. First, "it showed the country what was happening in the South and that made northern people put pressure—moral, ethical, and economic pressure—on the South to obey the rule of law. And, second, it shamed the southern people into realizing what was happening."[9]

In the 1940s, Gunnar Myrdal wrote about how change for African Americans was possible. In *An American Dilemma: The Negro Problem and Modern Democracy*, he wrote, "To get publicity is of the highest strategic importance to the Negro people." If the northern, mainstream press covered the southern racial story, the rest of the nation would be "shocked and shaken" and demand change.[10] *Life* offered that coverage. But with that coverage also came other perceptions of African Americans. As Kozol wrote in "Gazing at Race in the Pages of *Life*: Picturing Segregation Through Theory and History," there are numerous ways to interpret and "see" photographs. She wrote that *Life* "produced ways of seeing that ultimately condemned the worst practices of Jim Crow." However, by showing photographs of African Americans in this manner, the magazine also restricted "racial discourse."[11] In other words, by drawing attention to the plight of African Americans and the events surrounding the fight for civil rights, less attention was given to covering African Americans as average or middle-class, such as in the promotion of the ideals of the American family. With that being said, *Life* may have missed the opportunity to portray African Americans in everyday, normal activities but did raise the awareness of their dilemma in American society.

Life not only covered the civil rights movement with telling stories and powerful photographs, it also played a large part in showing the world the face of racism. It also promoted the status quo and negative stereotypes of African Americans: from 1937 with the photograph of a "mammy" eating watermelon to 1956 with a photograph of African-Americans inmates working on a chain gang (see Image 2.3).[12] Throughout its thirty-six year run as a weekly, the magazine covered civil rights–related events with enthusiasm and purpose but, at the same time, failed to show how a race of people lived and worked in a society dominated by whiteness; in other words, it did not show normal life for African Americans as it did so thoroughly with white America.

What *Life* did achieve, and what this study shows, was how a publication documented a struggle by a race of people over time and space. *Life* magazine presented the battle for civil rights as a moral, political, legal, and social battle, as well as a battle over space and the right to occupy that space.

Chapter 6

THE LANDSCAPE OF THE CIVIL RIGHTS MOVEMENT

Conflict of space has always been a part of our history and the events that defined that history. From the Revolutionary War, when early American settlers fought for the right to decide their political and geographic destiny, to the Civil War, when southern states seceded from the union, again for the ability to control their environment, the idea of having power over place has been with American culture for centuries. Who owns or controls space, private or public, political or social, physical or metaphysical, imagined or symbolic, has the power to influence, change, and direct the future in the case of the civil rights movement. The space where social action occurred—the protests, the marches, and the demonstrations—was a battlefield on many levels. Geographer Gillian Rose questioned the distinction between "real" and "non-real" spaces by arguing, "No space is free from human intent, human desire, and human imagination."[13] Geographer James Tyner wrote the study of space is "well positioned to contribute to an understanding of racism and other forms of injustice" but not in the traditional "empirical investigation of the social conditions in ghettos" or "another map of malnutrition, poverty, or crime."[14] He pointed out Robin Kelley's belief that "the conditions and the existence of social movements enable participants to imagine something different, to realize that things need not always be this way."[15] Thus, imagination and realization helped to institute change.

What *Life* did so well and so acutely was to document the events of the civil rights movement as the contention of space. Through the eyes of its photographers and editors, week after week, article after article, it showed readers the injustices inflicted upon African Americans in a physical and metaphysical way. Space was divided unequally, and the magazine graphically depicted that divide. Beginning with photographs of school integration in Hoxie, Arkansas, in 1955, with young school children waiting to register on their first day, the divide was shown. Six young African-American children were shown standing against a wall, nervous and timid, waiting to start their day, as white children moved freely around them. The image showed the children among other students but isolated in their own space, unprotected and vulnerable. Throughout the article, the photographs visually continue the idea of divided space, but ended with a positive scene. The last image depicted two African-American girls walking together with two white girls, arm in arm. The idea of integrated schools was shown as an alternative, more positive outcome. The story, framed in the title "A 'Morally Right' Decision," explained why integration could and would work.[16]

In September 1956, *Life* published stories on schools throughout the South that had been successfully integrated. Places like Clinton, Tennessee; Frankfurt, Kentucky; and Glen Burnie, Maryland; had problems, but the pictures showed students playing jump rope together, saying the

Pledge of Allegiance together, and holding hands while they square danced together. As Kozol noted, audiences read, see, and interpret photographs differently. While a photograph of square dancing in gym class might be interpreted as the first step in interracial marriage, it also might be seen as an innocent and healthy beginning of equal rights. African-American and white students occupying the same space without disagreement, violence, or tension was an innocuous yet powerful image. Examples of students harmonizing filled the pages of *Life* throughout the 1950s and 1960s.

As times changed and civil rights events became more violent and contentious, the magazine continued to emphasize space and relations. In May 1961, the story of the Freedom Rides through Alabama and Mississippi illustrated the purposeful and deliberate action to claim space that was controlled and negotiated by white segregationists. The photograph of an injured passenger and a burning Trailways bus on the side of the road became the consequences of African Americans pushing to take back that space.

Moore's photograph of off-duty deputies, preparing for a riot at the University of Mississippi in October 1962, was another example of the fight for space, although on a different level (see Image 4.5). This image, while putting a face on racism, became more symbolic and more emotionally loaded than previous photographs. The power of Moore's image epitomizes the deep divide between the races. In *Sons of Mississippi: A Story of Race and Its Legacy*, Paul Hendrickson described the image as "a lynching narrative," drawing emotional power from the Emmett Till murder and a history of intimidation and terror.[17] The expressions of delight on the faces of the deputies bring to mind a frenetic display of enthusiasm. That, and an understanding of the reasons behind such excitement, brings the photograph to a disturbing interpretation. The editors of *Life* understood how powerful the image was by publishing it across two full pages, allowing readers to see its impact. The editors understood that Moore's photographs were powerful and influential.

In May 1963, the editors once again showcased Moore's work from Birmingham with the image of firefighters using a fire hose on protesters (see Image 1.1). The sidewalk, a public space open to all, became the site of an authoritarian local government.[18] The space being fought for was both literal and figurative. African Americans, and people of all races, understood the connotations that the photograph showed. The oppressors could have been from any government or regime, while the oppressed also could have been from any minority group in history.

Moore's successive images of snarling police dogs and placid protesters succeeded on another level. In the photographs, the oppressors were law-enforcement officers and their dogs, while the victims were the African-American demonstrators (see Image 5.1).[19] The images became iconic and symbolic of an oppressed race in a wealthy country. They were, and continue to be, reproduced and discussed in regards to the American civil rights movement. They helped to change the course of civil rights legislation as Senator Jacob Javits stated in 1965.[20]

Another powerful image, published in December 1964, depicted Sheriff Lawrence Rainey and his deputy, Cecil Price. The two officers were being arraigned for the murders of Andrew Goodman, Michael Schwerner, and James Chaney in Meridian, Mississippi. The smiles on their faces during the proceedings were reminiscent of the off-duty deputies in Moore's 1963 photograph.[21] Both images depicted subjects that were jovial and carefree, which seemed unusual for the situation. Their smiles and complacency pervaded the space within the actual image.

The final article examined, regarding the contention of space and civil rights, was the March to Selma. The photographs, published in March 1965, showed the brutality by Alabama state troopers as they charged and clubbed peaceful marchers. The last bastion of political space, that of voting rights, was fought on the Edmund Pettus Bridge.

The incident in Selma that March was significant for another reason: television played a larger and more influential role in that incident than newspapers or magazines. Along with the photographers for *Life* and other print publications, television cameras also caught the brutal beatings. By this time in 1965, television had established itself as a powerful and lucrative medium, with an estimated seventy million television sets in fifty million American homes. In *The Life Cycles of Magazines*, A. J. Zuilen estimated that the annual volume of advertising revenue was $2.5 billion for the television industry as compared to $1 billion for magazines in 1965.[22]

Gene Roberts and Hank Klibanoff explained that while CBS and NBC covered the event, its impact would be greatest on ABC, which interrupted its Sunday Night Movie for fifteen minutes of footage from the beatings. The movie on that night was *Judgment at Nuremberg*, a "dramatic study of how the Germans had ignored, or acquiesced in, the horrors of Nazism." They wrote, "Suddenly viewers were watching—not Nazi Germany but segregationist Alabama. The juxtaposition struck like psychological lightning in American homes. Sheriff Clark's voice could be heard directing his posse: 'Get those goddamned niggers. And get those goddamned white niggers.'"[23]

Television had made an impact deeper than any magazine could. This was indicated by television's monumental rise in popularity from 1952 onward and the demise of general interest news magazines, such as *Life* and *Look*. Zuilen wrote that during the 1950s and 1960s, "television developed into an enemy of the mass audience magazines by siphoning away advertising revenues, which had kept, until that period, the American general interest mass audience magazines healthy and financially successful and profitable."[24] *Life*'s final issue as a weekly magazine was published on December 29, 1972. Today, every page of every issue of *Life* has been digitally scanned and can be found on the Internet through Google Books.

One concept of space, which was not mentioned, but was critical in every photograph, was the physical placement of the photographer; that is, where the photographer stood when they took the picture. Working photographers constantly thought about which vantage point would best describe the scene, where the light was coming from, and what elements enhanced or detracted from the composition of the image. In Birmingham, Moore placed himself in the center of the action and photographed with short, wide-angle lenses. By actively choosing to photograph in this manner, his images brought viewers into the scene. That was one reason why his dramatic images rose above other photographers.

The other aspect of space, which was equally important, was access. Photographers knew that without access to the right people or a church or a school, they would be unable to take meaningful pictures. Both Moore and Schulke had a relationship with Martin Luther King and had access to many of the behind-the-scene private moments, which allowed them the opportunity to take such poignant and powerful images. These ideas are fundamentally basic concepts to all photographers. Experienced photographers understand a situation, anticipate the possibilities of what might happen, and place themselves in an ideal spot to capture the most telling moments. In referring to photographers covering civil rights events, Wingo said, "When a photographer closes in on the action in a story, he/she is almost by definition choosing to seek some things and not others."[25] The vantage point from which a photograph was taken, was as important if not more than the moment itself. Space and placement becomes everything.

What *Life* did best was tell compelling stories with pictures. As Wilson Hicks wrote in his 1952 book, *Words and Pictures*, the goal was to "induce a phenomenon wherein the total of the complex—that is, picture and words together—becomes greater than the sum of its parts."[26] From its first publication on November 23, 1936, *Life* set itself apart from other pictorial, news, and general interest publications.

The question of the magazine's involvement and influence in the promotion of civil rights does not have a simple answer. The editors and photographers certainly believed they were on the right side of history, and they were. Schulke wrote, "There are times where the story is such and you understand what is happening that you become an advocate, . . . and I'm perfectly proud of being an advocate at that time. I think it's better for a photographer to have a point of view in a sociological story than to come into it cold and make good pictures."[27]

Stolley also believed in the virtue of the magazine. He recalled in 2011:

> *Life* was an advocate on its editorial pages. On the news pages, we tried to show both sides, or at least to give the segregationists a podium. One

of the problems back then was that [they] would often not speak to or cooperate with us. The other side was, of course, totally cooperative.... By *Life* inserting itself big time into the race story, [it] could not help but make the magazine an advocate, if only because showing the often violent defiance of the law of the land was certain to upset and anger a lot of the Americans. Which of course it did, and why moderate and reasonable southerners quickly saw the ultimate futility of their opposition to desegregation and [support of] Jim Crow.[28]

Wingo believed in the magazine as well, although he did not feel that *Life*'s function was as the journal of record, such as *The New York Times*. "Certainly *Life* did not feel it necessary to give the Klan's point of view when it reported the terrible things the Klan was doing in the desegregation struggle," he said. In 2011, when asked if *Life* was an advocate for the civil rights movement, Wingo answered:

I can attest that the managing editor of the magazine felt strongly, personally that *Life* had a responsibility to shake up the American people to the kind of things going on in the struggle, particularly where lives were lost or threatened by the opposition to civil rights. When I went to Philadelphia, Mississippi, after the 18 white men were indicted for the murder of Chaney, Schwerner and Goodman, the picture that *Life* chose to run as a double truck was of those men at their arraignment, sitting around laughing, chewing Red Man tobacco and looking for all the world like they knew they didn't have a thing to worry about. Sadly, they were right, but *Life* also was right in showing such arrogant bigotry and contempt for human life on the laughing faces of those men.[29]

Even with such high praise, the magazine missed a profound opportunity, an opportunity of inclusion. This study examined every issue of *Life* from January 1954 to December 1965 and coded every civil rights–related photograph and article. It also noted every photograph and advertisement containing an African American. African Americans were seen most in entertainment and sports-related stories. There were a few instances of African Americans in the background of photographs, portrayed as servants or laborers, and even fewer examples of African Americans shown in average, everyday settings: having dinner as a family, enjoying themselves at a Little League baseball game, or working as an employee other than in manual labor. The opportunity missed by *Life* and its editors was to show African Americans as equals in everyday life. In showing African Americans at some of their lowest points and as victims, they perpetuated the status quo of a white, middle-class, and consumer-driven society.

CONCLUSION

Life magazine published some of the most powerful and dramatic images of the civil rights movement, helping to push the fight for justice into the public discourse. It is not possible to know the specific impact of those images on the laws governing the nation or even with societal change. What is known is that *Life* magazine was a powerful force, both among the media and among its readers, for establishing the images of a nation dealing with deeply entrenched racial attitudes.

The issue of racial strife played out on the pages of *Life* for more than three decades. This study examined a twelve-year time frame, from 1954 to 1965, analyzing a representative sample of the stories and photographs published in the magazine as the nation debated over an essential question: What space should Africans Americans occupy in what *Life*'s Publisher Henry Luce called the "American century?" This study found that the magazine was both a leader and follower in that debate, publishing photographs that intimately recorded the battle for space on a variety of levels: on a physical level in images of school integration; on a metaphorical level with images of intimidation; and on a symbolic level with images describing the fight for equal rights in the streets of the South.

This study did not examine the editorial process behind what readers saw. Yet, it would not be a stretch to conclude that Luce was an integral voice in shaping the content of the magazine. Even though he was not physically present, his editors, such as Wilson Hicks noted in his book, felt his presence looming over them. What was apparent from the pages of the magazine was that in many cases, including *Life*'s five-part series on segregation in 1956, the visual narratives were carefully crafted from a wide variety of sources, sometimes from staff assignments, sometimes from wire photographs, and sometimes from both contract and freelance photographers.

In order to place *Life*'s coverage into context with other publications, a study of other national magazines and newspapers, such as *Time*, *Newsweek*, *Look*, *The Washington Post*, and *The New York Times*, would be necessary. Also, a more extensive examination of space devoted to other stories in *Life* would speak to the scope of civil rights–related coverage within the magazine.

On the surface, *Life* portrayed a street-level battle for fixing historic injustices. But, on another level, which spatial and geographic theory helps us to understand, *Life* magazine revealed a much deeper, ongoing debate over the rightful place of the African American in American society. Would they be equal with whites? Or, would they simply continue to be treated as second-class citizens? *Life*'s coverage, as this study showed, tended toward the latter, a visual narrative that cried out less for equality and more for simple humanity.

As the nation moves forward and the media landscape shifts and changes with new technology, this kind of study is essential in understanding what is being shown and what is not being presented in the media. Are the new titans of news merely crafting new narratives of humanity, or are they revealing invisible truths about the physical and metaphysical space occupied every day by their readers and viewers?

NOTES

1. See Steven Kasher, *The Civil Rights Movement: A Photographic History, 1954–68* (New York: Abbeville Press, 1996), 121; *Reporting Civil Rights, Part Two: American Journalism 1963–1973* (New York: Library of America, 2003), 27–28; and George Lewis, *Massive Resistance: The White Response to the Civil Rights Movement* (London: Hodder Arnold, 2006), 169–170.
2. Telephone interview, Hal Wingo, January 8, 2011.
3. Jennifer Podis, "Flip Schulke: A Photojournalist's Advocacy for the Southern Civil Rights Movement" (Master's thesis, University of Michigan, 1988), 44.
4. Leigh Raiford, *Imprisoned in a Luminous Glare: Photography and the African American Freedom Struggle* (Chapel Hill: University of North Carolina Press, 2011), 1–2.
5. Wendy Kozol, *Life's America: Family and Nation in Postwar Photojournalism* (Philadelphia: Temple University Press, 1994), 8.
6. Ibid.
7. Telephone interview, Richard B. Stolley, December 30, 2010.
8. The author examined issues of *Time* and *Newsweek* magazines on microfilm from September 16, 1957, to October 21, 1957. The issues looked at were September 16, September 23, September 30, October 7, October 14, and October 21 for both *Time* and *Newsweek*.
9. Telephone interview, Richard B. Stolley, December 30, 2010.
10. Gunnar Myrdal, *An American Dilemma: The Negro Problem and Modern Democracy* (New York: Harper & Row, 1962), 48.
11. Wendy Kozol, "Gazing at Race in the Pages of *Life*: Picturing Segregation through Theory and History," in Erika Lee Doss, ed., *Looking at Life Magazine* (Washington, D.C.: Smithsonian Institution Press, 2001), 173.
12. See "Watermelons to Harvest," *Life*, August 3, 1936, 52; and Robert Wallace, "The Voices of the White South," *Life*, September 17, 1956, 111.
13. Don Mitchell, *Cultural Geography: A Critical Introduction* (Oxford, England: Blackwell Publishers, 2000), 214.
14. James A. Tyner, *The Geography of Malcolm X: Black Radicalism and the Remaking of American Space* (New York: Routledge, 2006), 5–6.
15. Ibid., 8.
16. "A 'Morally Right' Decision," *Life*, July 25, 1955, 29–31.
17. Paul Hendrickson, *Sons of Mississippi: A Story of Race and Its Legacy* (New York: Alfred A. Knopf, 2003), 161.
18. "They Fight a Fire That Won't Go Out," *Life*, May 17, 1963, 28–37.
19. Ibid.
20. Michael S. Durham and Charles Moore, *Powerful Days: The Civil Rights Photography of Charles Moore* (New York: Stewart, Tabori & Chang, 1991), 32.
21. "Day of Accusation in Mississippi," *Life*, December 18, 1964, 34–35.
22. A. J. Zuilen, *The Life Cycle of Magazines: A Historical Study of the Decline and Fall of the General Interest Mass Audience Magazine in the United States during the Period 1946–1972* (Uithoorn, Netherlands: Graduate Press, 1977), 141, 167.
23. Gene Roberts and Hank Klibanoff, *The Race Beat: The Press, the Civil Rights Struggle, and the Awakening of a Nation* (New York: Knopf, 2006), 386.

24. Zuilen, *The Life Cycle of Magazines*, 2.
25. Telephone interview, Hal Wingo, January 8, 2011.
26. Wilson Hicks, *Words and Pictures* (New York: Arno Press, 1952), 6.
27. Podis, "Flip Schulke," 62.
28. Email correspondence, Richard B. Stolley, April 16, 2011.
29. Email correspondence, Hal Wingo, April 16, 2011.

References

BOOKS

Anderson, Sherwood. *Home Town*. New York: Alliance Book Corp, 1940.

Baughman, James L. *Henry R. Luce and the Rise of the American News Media*. Boston: Twayne Publishers, 1987.

Branch, Taylor. *Parting the Waters: America in the King Years, 1954–63*. New York: Simon and Schuster, 1989.

Brinkley, Alan. *The Publisher: Henry Luce and His American Century*. New York: Alfred A. Knopf, 2010.

Cagin, Seth, and Philip Dray. *We Are Not Afraid: The Story of Goodman, Schwerner, and Chaney and the Civil Rights Campaign for Mississippi*. New York: Macmillan Pub. Co., 1988.

Chafe, William Henry, Raymond Gavins, and Robert Rodgers Korstad. *Remembering Jim Crow: African Americans Tell about Life in the Segregated South*. New York: New Press, 2001.

Chapnick, Howard. *Truth Needs No Ally: Inside Photojournalism*. Columbia: University of Missouri Press, 1994.

Coles, Robert. *Doing Documentary Work*. New York: New York Public Library, 1997.

Counts, I. Wilmer, Will D. Campbell, Ernest Dumas, and Robert S. McCord. *A Life Is More Than a Moment: The Desegregation of Little Rock's Central High*. Bloomington: Indiana University Press, 1999.

Cox, Julian. *Road to Freedom: Photographs of the Civil Rights Movement, 1956–1968*. Atlanta: High Museum of Art, 2008.

Daniel, Pete. *Lost Revolutions: The South in the 1950s*. Washington, D.C.; Chapel Hill: University of North Carolina Press, 2000.

Davis, George Arliss, and O. Donaldson. *Blacks in the United States: A Geographic Perspective*. Boston: Houghton Mifflin, 1975.

Doss, Erika Lee. *Looking at* Life *Magazine*. Washington, D.C.: Smithsonian Institution Press, 2001.

Durham, Michael S., and Charles Moore. *Powerful Days: The Civil Rights Photography of Charles Moore*. New York: Stewart, Tabori & Chang, 1991.

Dwyer, Owen J., and Derek H. Alderman. *Civil Rights Memorials and the Geography of Memory*. Chicago: University of Georgia Press, 2008.

Elliott, George P. *Dorothea Lange*. New York: Doubleday, 1966 (Catalog of an exhibition held at the Museum of Modern Art, New York).

Finnegan, Cara A. *Picturing Poverty: Print Culture and FSA Photographs*. Washington D.C.: Smithsonian Books, 2003.

Firth, Raymond, ed. *Man and Culture: An Evaluation of the Work of Bronislaw Malinowski*. London: Routledge & Kegan Paul, 1957.

Fisher, Paul L., and Ralph Lynn Lowenstein, eds., *Race and the News Media*. New York: Praeger, 1967.

Garrow, David J., ed. *The Walking City: The Montgomery Bus Boycott, 1955–1956*. Brooklyn, New York: Carlson Publishing Inc., 1989.

Geertz, Clifford. *The Interpretation of Cultures: Selected Essays*. New York: Basic Books, Inc., 1973.

Graham, Allison. *Framing the South: Hollywood, Television, and Race During the Civil Rights Struggle*. Baltimore: Johns Hopkins University Press, 2001.
Halberstam, David. *The Powers That Be*. New York: Knopf, 1979.
Hale, Grace Elizabeth. *Making Whiteness: The Culture of Segregation in the South, 1890–1940*. New York: Pantheon Books, 1998.
Hendrickson, Paul. *Sons of Mississippi: A Story of Race and Its Legacy*. New York: Alfred A. Knopf, 2003.
Herzstein, Robert Edwin. *Henry R. Luce, Time, and the American Crusade in Asia*. Cambridge, UK; New York: Cambridge University Press, 2005.
———. *Henry R. Luce: A Political Portrait of the Man Who Created the American Century*. New York: C. Scribner's Sons, 1994.
Hicks, Wilson. *Words and Pictures*. New York: Arno Press, 1952.
Houck, Davis W., and David E. Dixon. *Rhetoric, Religion and the Civil Rights Movement, 1954–1965*. Studies in Rhetoric and Religion. Vol. 1. Waco, Tex.: Baylor University Press, 2006.
Hurley, F. Jack. *Portrait of a Decade: Roy Stryker and the Development of Documentary Photography in the Thirties*. Baton Rouge: Louisiana State University Press, 1972.
Kasher, Steven. *The Civil Rights Movement: A Photographic History, 1954– 68*. New York: Abbeville Press, 1996.
King, Martin Luther. *Why We Can't Wait*. New York: New American Library, 1964.
Kozol, Wendy. *Life's America: Family and Nation in Postwar Photojournalism*. Philadelphia: Temple University Press, 1994.
La Farge, John. *The Race Question and the Negro: A Study of the Catholic Doctrine on Interracial Justice*. New York; Toronto: Longmans, Green and Co., 1943.
LeBeau, Bryan F. *Currier & Ives: America Imagined*. Washington, D.C.: Smithsonian Institution Press, 2001.
Lentz, Richard. *Symbols, the News Magazines, and Martin Luther King*. Baton Rouge: Louisiana State University Press, 1990.
Levy, Peter B. *The Civil Rights Movement*. Westport, Conn.: Greenwood Press, 1998.
———, ed. *Let Freedom Ring: Documentary History of the Modern Civil Rights Movement*. New York: Greenwood Press, 1992.
Lewis, George. *Massive Resistance: The White Response to the Civil Rights Movement*. London: Hodder Arnold, 2006.
Loengard, John. *Life Photographers: What They Saw*. Boston: Little, Brown, and Company, 1998.
Martindale, Carolyn. *The White Press and Black America*. New York: Greenwood Press, 1986.
McDannell, Colleen. *Picturing Faith: Photography and the Great Depression*. New Haven, Conn.: Yale University Press, 2004.
McKittrick, Katherine, and Clyde Adrian Woods. *Black Geographies and the Politics of Place*. Toronto, Ont.: Between the Lines, 2007.
Mitchell, Don. *Cultural Geography: A Critical Introduction*. Oxford, UK: Blackwell Publishers, 2000.
———. *The Right to the City: Social Justice and the Fight for Public Space*. New York: Guilford Press, 2003.
Morris, John G. *Get the Picture: A Personal History of Photojournalism*. New York: Random House, 1998.
Mott, Frank Luther. *American Journalism: A History, 1690–1960*, 3rd ed. New York: The MacMillan Company, 1962.
Myrdal, Gunnar. *An American Dilemma: The Negro Problem and Modern Democracy*. New York: Harper & Row, 1962.
National Association for the Advancement of Colored People. *NAACP Civil Rights Handbook*. New York: National Association for the Advancement of Colored People, 1973.
Newman, Mark. *The Civil Rights Movement*. Edinburgh: Edinburgh University Press, 2004.

Parks, Gordon. *A Choice of Weapons*. New York: Harper & Row, 1966.
———. *Moments Without Proper Names*. New York: Viking Press, 1975.
———. *To Smile in Autumn: A Memoir*. Minneapolis: University of Minnesota Press, 2009.
Parks, Gordon, and Maren Stange, *Bare Witness: Photographs*. Milan: Skira, 2006.
Raeburn, John. *A Staggering Revolution: A Cultural History of Thirties Photography*. Chicago: University of Illinois Press, 2006.
Raiford, Leigh. *Imprisoned in a Luminous Glare: Photography and the African American Freedom Struggle*. Chapel Hill: University of North Carolina Press, 2011.
Rayfield, Stanley. Life *Photographers, Their Careers and Favorite Pictures*. Garden City, N.Y.: Doubleday, 1957.
Reporting Civil Rights, Part Two: America Journalism 1963–1973. New York: Library of America, 2003.
Roberts, Gene, and Hank Klibanoff. *The Race Beat: The Press, the Civil Rights Struggle, and the Awakening of a Nation*. New York: Knopf, 2006.
Rose, Gillian. *Visual Methodologies: An Introduction to the Interpretation of Visual Materials*. London; Thousand Oaks, Calif.: Sage, 2012.
Sandeen, Eric J. *Picturing an Exhibition: The Family of Man and 1950s America*. Albuquerque: University of New Mexico Press, 1995.
Sandler, Martin W. *America through the Lens: Photographers Who Changed the Nation*. New York: Henry Holt and Co., 2005.
Scherman, David Edward. *The Best of* Life. New York: Flare Books, 1975.
Schulke, Flip, and Matt Schudel. *Witness to Our Times: My Life as a Photojournalist*. Chicago: Cricket Books, 2003.
Shoemaker, Pamela J., and Stephen D. Reese. *Mediating the Message: Theories of Influences on Mass Media Content*. 2nd ed. White Plains, N.Y.: Longman, 1996.
Sibley, David. *Geographies of Exclusion: Society and Difference in the West*. London; New York: Routledge, 1995.
Simmons, Charles A. *The African American Press: A History of News Coverage during National Crises, with Special Reference to Four Black Newspapers, 1827–1965*. Jefferson, N.C.: McFarland & Co., 1998.
Steichen, Edward. *The Family of Man: The Greatest Photographic Exhibition of all Time*. New York: Museum of Modern Art, 1955.
Swanberg, W. A. *Luce and His Empire*. New York: Scribner, 1972.
Tyner, James A. *The Geography of Malcolm X: Black Radicalism and the Remaking of American Space*. New York: Routledge, 2006.
Washburn, Patrick Scott. *The African American Newspaper: Voice of Freedom*. Evanston, Ill.: Northwestern University Press, 2006.
Welky, David. *Everything Was Better in America: Print Culture in the Great Depression*. Urbana: University of Illinois Press, 2008.
Wexler, Sanford. *The Civil Rights Movement: An Eyewitness History*. New York: Facts on File, 1993.
Williams, Juan. *Eyes on the Prize: America's Civil Rights Years, 1954–1965*. New York: Viking, 1987.
Wright, Richard, and Edwin Rosskam. *12 Million Black Voices*. New York: Thunder's Mouth Press, 1941.
Zuilen, A. J. *The Life Cycle of Magazines: A Historical Study of the Decline and Fall of the General Interest Mass Audience Magazine in the United States during the Period 1946–1972*. Uithoorn, Netherlands: Graduate Press, 1977.

BOOK CHAPTERS

Berlier, Monique. "The Family of Man: Readings of an Exhibition." In Bonnie Brennen and Hanno Hardt. *Picturing the Past: Media, History, and Photography*. Urbana: University of Illinois Press, 1999.

Fuller, Jennifer. "Debating the Present Through the Past: Representations of the Civil Rights Movement in the 1990s." In Renee Christine Romano and Leigh Raiford. *The Civil Rights Movement in American Memory*. Athens: University of Georgia Press, 2006.

Myrdal, Gunnar. "The Racial Crisis in Perspective." In Armistead Scott Pride and Jack Lyle. *The Black American and the Press*. Los Angeles: W. Ritchie Press, 1968.

Weill, Susan M. "Mississippi's Daily Press in Three Crises." In David R. Davies. *The Press and Race: Mississippi Journalists Confront the Movement*. Jackson: University Press of Mississippi, 2001.

JOURNALS AND PERIODICALS

Delaney, David. "The Space That Race Makes." *The Professional Geographer* 54, no. 1 (February 2002): 6–14.

Dwyer, Owen J. "Interpreting the Civil Rights Movement: Place, Memory, and Conflict." *The Professional Geographer* 52, no. 4 (November 2000): 660–671.

Hariman, Robert, and John L. Lucaites. "Performing Civic Identity: The Iconic Photograph of the Flag Raising on Iwo Jima." *Quarterly Journal of Speech* 88 (November 2002): 363–392.

Hoelscher, Steven. "Making Place, Making Race: Performances of Whiteness in the Jim Crow South." *Annals of the Association of American Geographers* 93, no. 3 (September 2003): 657–686.

Johnson, Davi. "Martin Luther King Jr.'s 1963 Birmingham Campaign as Image Event." *Rhetoric & Public Affairs* 10, no. 1 (Spring 2007): 1–25.

Kaplan, John. "The *Life* Magazine Civil Rights Photography of Charles Moore 1958–1965." *Journalism History* 25, no. 4 (2000): 126.

Lester, Paul Martin. "African-American Photo Coverage in Four U.S. Newspapers, 1937–1990." *Journalism Quarterly* 71, no. 2 (Summer 1994): 380–394.

Lester, Paul Martin, and Ron Smith. "African-American Photo Coverage in *Life*, *Newsweek* and *Time*, 1937–1988." *Journalism Quarterly* 67, no. 1 (Spring 1990): 128–136.

Mendelson, Andrew. "Slice-of-Life Moments as Visual 'Truth.'" *Journalism History* 29, no. 4 (2004): 166–178.

Robnett, Belinda. "African-American Women in the Civil Rights Movement, 1954–1965: Gender, Leadership, and Micromobilization." *American Journal of Sociology* 101, no. 6 (May 1996): 1661.

Schwalbe, C. B. "Images of Brutality: The Portrayal of U.S. Racial Violence in News Photographs Published Overseas (1957–1963)." *American Journalism* 23, no. 4 (2006): 93–116.

Sentman, Mary Alice."Black and White: Disparity in Coverage by *Life* Magazine from 1937 to 1972." *Journalism Quarterly* 60, no. 3 (September 1983): 501–508.

Spratt, Meg. "When Police Dogs Attacked: Iconic News Photographs and Construction of History, Mythology, and Political Discourse." *American Journalism* 25, no. 2 (2008): 85–105.

Trodd, Zoe. "A Negative Utopia: Protest Memory and the Spatio-Symbolism of Civil Rights Literature and Photography." *African American Review* 42, no. 1 (Spring 2008): 25–40.

LIFE MAGAZINE

"A Bold Boycott Goes On." *Life*, March 5, 1946.
"A Head Start on Racial Equality." *Life*, May 31, 1954.
"A Historic Decision for Equality." *Life*, May 31, 1954.
"A Historic Week of Civil Strife." *Life*, October 7, 1957.
"A Morally Right Decision." *Life*, July 25, 1955.

"A Reason for Smiles in 'Back-of-Town.'" *Life*, March 29, 1954.
"A Remarkable Dinner and . . . Off to Jail." *Life*, February 12, 1965.
"A Roundtable as Debate on Christians' Moral Duty." *Life*, October 1, 1956.
"A Young Mob Tests a City." *Life*, October 11, 1954.
"An Encroaching Menace." *Life*, April 11, 1955.
"Angry Oratory in Mississippi." *Life*, June 20, 1955.
"Aroused Citizens Strike at Faubus." *Life*, June 8, 1959.
"Bloody Beatings, Burning Bus in the South." *Life*, May 6, 1961.
"Calm and Hopeful Integration Start." *Life*, February 16, 1959.
"Chief Counsel for Equality." *Life*, June 13, 1955.
"Claimants of Civil Equality Help Fight Own Battle." *Life*, September 19, 1960.
"Common Bonds of Man." *Life*, February 14, 1955.
Crawford, Marc. "The Ominous Malcolm X Exits from the Muslims." *Life*, March 20, 1964.
"Day of Accusation in Mississippi." *Life*, December 18, 1964.
"Death of Malcolm X and the Resulting Vengeful Gang War: A Monument to Negro Upheaval." *Life*, March 5, 1965.
"Emmett Till's Day in Court." *Life*, October 3, 1955.
Evers, Myrlie. "Arlington Receives a Murdered Hero." *Life*, June 28, 1963.
"Faubus Defiance of Federal Rule." *Life*, September 23, 1957.
"Fervent Faces Amid a Gathering of Pilgrims." *Life*, June 3, 1957.
"Flare-Up over a Sit-Down." *Life*, February 29, 1960.
"For Prayer, Pain." *Life*, March 28, 1960.
"Fuss over Integrated Black Bunny." *Life*, June 1, 1959.
Graham, Billy. "Billy Graham Makes Plea for an End to Intolerance." *Life*, October 1, 1956.
"Harlem Gang Leader." *Life*, November 1, 1948.
"Harlem's 'Long Hot Summer' Begins." *Life*, July 31, 1964.
"Homecoming of a Lynch Victim." *Life*, September 12, 1955.
"How It Feels to Be Beat Up by a Rampaging Mob." *Life*, April 3, 1964.
"How It Feels to Be Black." *Life*, August 16, 1963.
"In Memoriam, Emmett Till." *Life*, October 10, 1955.
"'Integration' in the South." *Life*, November 28, 1960.
"Lead Belly: Bad Nigger Makes Good Minstrel." *Life*, April 19, 1937.
"Legislative and Judicial Fronts for Civil Rights: Embattled White South Digs In." *Life*, July 22, 1957.
"Letters to the Editors." *Life*, March 1, 1937.
"Letters to the Editors." *Life*, October 24, 1938.
"Letters to the Editors." *Life*, November 22, 1948.
"Letters to the Editors." *Life*, July 11, 1955.
"Letters to the Editors." *Life*, August 15, 1955.
"Letters to the Editors." *Life*, October 24, 1955.
"Letters to the Editors." *Life*, November 28, 1955.
"Letters to the Editors." *Life*, March 12, 1956.
"Letters to the Editors." *Life*, March 26, 1956.
"Letters to the Editors." *Life*, October 8, 1956.
"Letters to the Editors." *Life*, October 7, 1957.
"Letters to the Editors." *Life*, October 13, 1957.
"Letters to the Editors." *Life*, June 7, 1963.
"Letters to the Editors." *Life*, July 19, 1963.
"Letters to the Editors." *Life*, September 27, 1963.
"Letters to the Editors." *Life*, April 9, 1965.
"Little Rock's Chief Stops the 'Seggies.'" *Life*, August 24, 1959.
Luce, Henry. "The American Century." *Life*, February 17, 1941.
"Lunch Counter Segregation Skirmish." *Life*, March 7, 1960.
"Maryland, My Maryland, the Bayonets and the Cameras Flash." *Life*, May 22, 1964.

Morgan, Charles, Jr. "Birmingham: An Alabaman's Great Speech Lays the Blame." *Life*, September 27, 1963.
"Negroes, The U.S. Also Has a Minority Problem." *Life*, October 3, 1938.
"One Lynching Spurs Congress to Stop Others." *Life*, April 26, 1937.
"Out of a Cauldron of Hate—Arson and Death." *Life*, August 27 1965.
"Picture of the Week." *Life*, October 5, 1962.
"Racial Fury over Sit-In." *Life*, September 12, 1960.
"Segregation's Celebrity 10 Years Later." *Life*, May 22, 1964.
"Segregationist Surrender." *Life*, February 9, 1959.
"Selma: Beatings Start the Savage Season." *Life*, March 19, 1965.
"South Worries over Miss Lucy." *Life*, February 20, 1956.
Stolley, Richard B. "A Sequel to Segregation." *Life*, December 10, 1956.
"Supreme Court Justices Hurry to a Historic Special Summer Session." *Life*, September 8, 1958.
"The Flood Leaves Its Victims on the Bread Line." *Life*, February 15, 1937.
"The Halting and Fitful Battle for Integration." *Life*, September 17, 1956.
"The Limpid Shambles of Violence." *Life*, July 3, 1964.
"The Lost Class of 1959." *Life*, November 3, 1958.
"The Nation Surges to Join the Negro on His March." *Life*, March 6, 1965.
"The Negro and the North." *Life*, March 11, 1957.
"The New Voting Law Goes into Action." *Life*, August 20, 1965.
"The Ride for Rights." *Life*, June 2, 1961.
"The Siege over Civil Rights." *Life*, March 14, 1960.
"The States Rights Issue." *Life*, September 23, 1957.
"The Violent End of the Man Called Malcolm." *Life*, March 5, 1965.
"The 'Whys' of Hate." *Life*, October 25, 1954.
"They Come Marching Up Conscience Road." *Life*, September 6, 1963.
"They Fight a Fire That Won't Go Out." *Life*, May 17, 1963.
"They Finally Did It: They Busted the Big Filibuster." *Life*, June 19, 1964.
"Troubles Beset School Opening." *Life*, September 16, 1957.
"US Troops Take Over in Arkansas." *Life*, October 7, 1957.
"Vital Verdict in the South." *Life*, August 5, 1957.
Wallace, Robert. "Freedom to Jim Crow." *Life*, September 10, 1956.
———. "How the Negro Came to Slavery in America." *Life*, September 3, 1956.
———. "The Restraints: Open and Hidden." *Life*, September 24, 1956.
———. "The Voices of the White South." *Life*, September 17, 1956.
"Watermelons to Harvest." *Life*, August 3, 1936.
"Whale of a Week of News." *Life*, February 22, 1960.
White, Theodore H. "Power Structure, Integration, Militancy, Freedom Now!" *Life*, November 29, 1963.
———. "Racial Collision in the Big Cities." *Life*, November 2, 1963.
"You Have Cried Enough Tears for Me." *Life*, October 10, 1955.

UNPUBLISHED SOURCES AND GOVERNMENT DOCUMENTS

Flamiano, Dolores. "African Americans in *Life*, 1936–1948: From Sensational Racism to Civil Rights." Convention paper, Birmingham, Alabama, 2009.
Gordon Parks Collection, Manuscript Division. Library of Congress, Washington, D.C.
Henry Robinson Luce Collection, Manuscript Division. Library of Congress, Washington, D.C.
Podis, Jennifer. "Flip Schulke: A Photojournalist's Advocacy for the Southern Civil Rights Movement." Master's thesis, University of Michigan, 1988.
Spruill, Larry Hawthorne. "Southern Exposure: Photography and the Civil Rights Movement, 1955–1968." Ph.D. dissertation, State University of New York at Stony Brook, 1983.

NEWSPAPERS

"Anti-lynching Bill Is Passed by House after Bitter Talk." *The New York Times*, April 16, 1937, 1.
"Copeland Sees Doom of Anti-lynching Bill." *The New York Times*, August 1, 1937, 2.
Phillips, Cabell. "Integration: Battle of Hoxie, Arkansas." *The New York Times Sunday Magzine*, September 25, 1955.

INTERVIEWS

Corn, Jack. Telephone interview by author, February 28, 2011. Tape recorded.
Schapiro, Steve. Telephone interview by author, February 8, 2011. Tape recorded.
Shay, Art. Telephone interview by author, February 20, 2011. Tape recorded.
Stolley, Richard B. Telephone interview by author, December 30, 2010. Tape recorded.
Wingo, Hal. Telephone interview by author, January 8, 2011. Tape recorded.

EMAIL CORRESPONDENCE

Email correspondence, Hal Wingo, April 16, 2011.
Email correspondence, Malcolm O. Carpenter, July 21, 2016.
Email correspondence, Richard B. Stolley, April 16, 2011.

Index

Aaron, Julia, 78
Abbott, Robert Sengstacke, 19. *See also Chicago Defender*
ABC television station, 92, 112
Alabama state troopers, 100, 112
Allen, Ivan, Jr., Atlanta mayor, 98
Almond, Lindsay, Virginia governor, 69, 70
American civil rights movement, 1, 6, 112
"American Gothic" photograph, 13
American Society of Magazine Photographers, 1
Anderson, Sherwood, 15
Anniston, Alabama, 77
Anniston Star, Anniston, Alabama, 77
Arista, West Virginia, 44
Arkansas Democrat, 67, 68
Arkansas legislature, 69
Arkansas National Guard, 59, 63, 65
Arkansas State Press, 64. *See also* black press
Arlington National Cemetery, 90
Ashmore, Harry S., 70
Atlanta Constitution, 20
Atlanta, Georgia, 97–98

Barnett, Ross, Mississippi governor, 40, 79
Bates, Daisy, 64, 65
Baughman, James L., 27
Bennett, Freddy, 102
Berlier, Monique, 39
Birmingham, Alabama, 43, 78, 88, 107; fire department, 88; protest movement in, 1, 2, 3, 6, 10, 87, 88–90, 91, 111
Birmingham News, Birmingham, Alabama, 75
Black Muslims, 99

black nationalism, 99
black press, 9, 18–20. *See also Arkansas State Press*; *Chicago Defender*; *Freedom's Journal*; Negro Newspaper Publishers Association; *Pittsburgh Courier*; *Tri-State Defender*; Washburn, Patrick S.
black reconstruction, 99
Black Star photo agency, 2, 55n8, 89, 100. *See also* Schulke, Flip; Moore, Charles; Tenney, Gordon
Booker, Simeon, 28
Bourke-White, Margaret, 8, 22, 23, 26, 44, 49; photograph by, 23, 51
Bradley, Mamie, 40, 42
Briggs, Harry, Jr., 37
Brown Chapel African Methodist Episcopal Church, Selma, Alabama, 100
Brown, Linda, 37, 94. *See also* Smith, Linda Brown
Brown v. Board of Education, 3, 28, 33, 34–38, 41, 46, 54, 61, 72, 94, 108
Brownsville, Tennessee, 76
Bryan, Hazel, 63–65
Bryant, Carolyn, 41, 43
Bryant, Roy, 40, 42
Bryson, John, 66
Burgert, A. P.: photograph by, 22

Cagan, Seth, 97
Carmichael, Stokely, 95
Carpenter, Malcolm O., 73–74; photograph by, 68
Carter, Esther, U.S. commissioner, 97
Cass, Kenneth, Greenville (South Carolina) mayor, 50
Causey, Allie Lee, 52–54, 75
Causey, Shirley, 54
Causey, Willie, 52–54, 75

Index

CBS television station, 92, 112
Central High School, Little Rock, Arkansas, 9, 10, 55, 59, 62, 64, 66, 68, 70, 108
Chaney, James, 85–86, 95, 112, 114
Chapnick, Howard, 27
Charleston, South Carolina, 47
Charlotte, North Carolina, 62, 63
Chicago Defender, 19. *See also* Abbott, Robert Sengstacke; black press
Chicago Tribune, 20
Christ the King School, Orangeburg, South Carolina, 36
Civil Rights Act of 1964, 1, 10, 81, 86, 94
Civil Rights Handbook, 5, 11n15, 34, 55n12, 64
Civil War, 47, 49, 110
Clark, Edward, 41, 44, 49, 70, 112; photograph by, 42
Claymont High School, Claymont, Delaware, 37
Clinton, Tennessee, 44–45, 66, 110
Cloud, Major John, 100
Coca-Cola Company, 98
Collins, Sarah Jean, 93
Commission of Inquiry on Freedom of the Press, 27
compositional interpretation, 5, 11n16, 60. *See also* Rose, Gillian Rosemary
Connor, Theophilus Eugene "Bull," 2, 78, 88, 89
contested space, 6, 46, 47, 61, 62, 65, 67, 69, 71, 76, 77, 86, 88, 98, 99, 110, 111
Corley, Bob, 75
Counts, Dorothy, 62, 63, 66
Counts, Will, 65, 67; photograph by, 68
Crane, Ralph, 49
Cravens, Don, 43, 46, 53
cultural landscape, 6, 18. *See also* Mitchell, Donald
Currier and Ives, 48

Dallas County, Alabama, 99
Dandridge, Frank, 93, 105n26
Delaney, David, 7
De Marisco, Dick : photograph by, 96
Demopolis, Alabama, 103
Dennis, David, 78

Dirksen, Everett, Senate minority leader, 94
Doss, Erika Lee, 21–22, 24, 25, 26
Double V Campaign, 18–19
Dray, Philip, 97
Duck Hill, Mississippi, 40
Durham, Michael S., 79, 87, 94

East Louisiana Railroad Company, 17
Easton, Maryland, 62, 66
Eckford, Elizabeth, 59, 63–65, 71
Edey, Maitland A., 8, 92
Edmund Pettus Bridge, Selma, Alabama, 81, 99–102, 112
Eisenhower, Dwight D., 38, 65, 66, 67
Eisenstaedt, Alfred, 24, 26
Ellender, Alan, Louisiana senator, 94
Ellington, Duke, 25
Elliot, George P., 8
Elsmere, Kentucky, 45
Evans, Angeline "Angie," 69
Evers, James Van, 90
Evers, Medgar, 87, 90–91
Evers, Myrlie Louise, 90

"Family of Man," 38, 39
Farm Security Administration (FSA), 13–16
Faubus, Orval Eugene, Arkansas governor, 10, 55, 61, 62, 63, 65, 67, 69, 70
Faulkner, William, 47; and family, 49
Ferrell, Billy, 80
Fine, Benjamin, 59, 65
Fisk University, 77
Flamiano, Delores, 22, 24, 25, 26
Folsom, Jim, Alabama governor, 47
Fortune, 26
Foucault, Michael, 61
Frankfort, Kentucky, 45, 110
Freedom Rides, 10, 55, 61, 77–78, 111
Freedom's Journal, 19. *See also* black press
Freedom Summer, 10, 28, 85

Gavagan anti-lynching bill, 40
Gillespie Park School, Greensboro, North Carolina, 63
Glen Burnie, Maryland, 45, 110

Goodman, Andrew, 85–86, 95, 112, 114
Graham, Allison, 33
Graham, Billy, 54
Granby High School, Norfolk, Virginia, 70
Great Depression, 13
Greensboro, North Carolina, 62, 63, 72
Greenville, South Carolina, 51

Halberstam, David, 27
Hale, Grace Elizabeth, 17
Harding High School, Charlotte, North Carolina, 62, 63
Hariman, Robert, 88
Harlem gang, 25
Harlem Renaissance, 24
Hearst, William Randolph, 19
Hendrickson, Paul, 40, 80, 111
Hershorn, Shel, 69
Herzstein, Robert Edwin, 26
Hicks, Wilson, 8, 12n33, 24, 25, 113
Hoelscher, Steve D., 7
Home News, Montgomery, Alabama, 71
Hoxie, Arkansas, 33, 34, 38, 40, 110
Huie, William Bradford, 43
Humphrey, Hubert, democratic whip, 94
Hunt, George, 107
Hutchins, Robert M., 27

iconic photographs, 88
integration. *See* school integration
Inter-Racial Fellowship General Assembly of the Presbyterian Church, 28
Interstate Commerce Commission, 78

Jack, Wellborn, state representative, 76
Jackson, Leonard "Red," 25
Jackson, Mahalia, 91
Jackson, Mississippi, 91
Jacksonville, Florida, 94
Javits, Jacob Koppel, 1, 88, 111
Jenkins, Johnny, 64; photograph by, 64
Jet magazine, 28
Jim Crow laws, 17, 49, 109, 114
Johnson, Davi, 3
Johnson, Frank M., U.S. judge, 101

Johnson, Lyndon B., 85, 93, 97, 102, 105n27
Johnson, Paul, Mississippi lieutenant governor, 80
Jones, Charlie, 103
Jones, Robert, 75
Judgement at Nuremberg, 112

Kasher, Steven, 8, 46, 72, 85, 103
Kelley, Robert W., 36, 43, 44; photograph by, 45
Kennedy, John F., 76, 77, 79, 90, 105n27; assassination of, 93
Kennedy, Robert F., 79
King, Dexter Scott, 98
King, Martin Luther III, 98
King, Martin Luther, Jr., 1, 2, 43, 46, 90, 91–92, 94, 95, 97–98, 99, 104, 113; "I have a dream" speech by, 92; power of photography, knowing the, 108
King, Yolanda Denise, 98
Klibanoff, Hank, 2, 17, 43, 65, 67, 92, 98, 102, 112
Kodak Crystal Eagle Award, 10n3
Kozol, Wendy, 8, 20, 47, 49, 50, 51, 54, 108, 109, 110
Ku Klux Klan, 49, 78, 85, 102, 114

Lange, Dorothea, 8
Lawson, James, Jr., 78
Ledbetter, Huddie William "Lead Belly," 21
Lentz, Richard, 46, 95
Lester, Paul Martin, 20
Levy, Maurice, 78
Levy, Peter B., 36, 93, 94, 104
Lewis, George, 77
Lewis, John, 100
Life magazine, 2, 7, 20, 26, 55, 107, 109, 112, 113, 114, 115; circulation, 8, 26, 27, 60, 82n6, 115; cultural reportage, 27; final issue, 112; first issue, 26; prospectus of 1936, 21, 108; stereotypes, 21, 22, 24, 95
Little Rock Nine, 10, 59, 61, 62–68
Liuzzo, Viola, 102
Loengard, John, 90
Look magazine, 43, 108, 112, 115

Louisville, Kentucky : flood of 1937, 22, 23
Lucaites, John L., 88
Luce, Elizabeth Root, 26
Luce, Henry Robinson, 7, 9, 21, 22, 26, 27–29, 115; "American century," 115
Luce, Henry Winters, 26
Lucy, Autherine Juanita, 43
lynching, 39–40, 49

Malcolm X, 94; assassination of, 98–99
Mansfield, Texas, 44
March on Washington, D.C., 10, 87, 91
Marshall, Thurgood, 38
Martindale, Carolyn, 20
Maryland Historical magazine, 13
Maury High School, Norfolk, Virginia, 69
McClellan, John, Arkansas senator, 94
McCombe, Leonard, 8
McDaniel, "Bootjack," 40
McMahon, Franklin, 41
McShane, James, Chief U.S. Marshal, 79
Mellichamp Elementary School, Orangeburg, South Carolina, 36
Mendelson, Andrew. *See* photographic style
Meredith, James, 79–81
Meridian, Mississippi, 85, 97, 112
Meridian Star (Mississippi), 97
Milam, J. W., 41–43
Miller, Francis, 59, 66, 71, 75, 105n26
Miller, Wayne, 39
Mitchell, Donald, 6, 18, 86, 88
Mobile, Alabama, 52
Moffett, Hugh, 53
Mohammed, Elijah, 99
Money, Mississippi, 28, 40, 41
Montgomery bus boycott, 46–47
Moore, Charles, 1, 6, 79, 80, 87, 89–90, 94, 99, 102, 105n26, 111, 113; photograph by, 2, 81, 89, 100
Morgan, Charles, Jr., 93
Mount Zion Methodist Church, Longdale, Mississippi, 85
Museum of Modern Art, 38, 39
Myrdal, Gunnar, 16, 18, 109

Natchez, Mississippi, 7
Nation of Islam, 98
National Association for the Advancement of Colored People (NAACP), 46, 64, 90
Nazism, 112
NBC television station, 92, 112
Negro Newspaper Publishers Association, 20. *See also* black press
Neshoba County, Mississippi, 85, 95
Newsweek magazine, 12n40, 20, 59, 82n4, 95, 108, 115
New York City riots, 95, 96, 98
New York Times, 20, 65, 92, 114, 115
New York World Telegraph and Sun, 96
Nixon, Richard M., 76
Nobel Peace Prize, 97–98
Norcom High School, Portsmouth, Virginia, 73
North Carolina Agricultural and Technical College, 72
Norview High School, Norfolk, Virginia, 69

Omaha, Nebraska, 49

Parks, Gordon, 9, 13–16, 25, 26, 52, 87, 99, 105n26
Parks, Rosa, 28, 43, 46
Philadelphia, Mississippi, 10, 85, 114
Phillips, Cabell, 33
photographic essay, 8, 12n34, 27, 92
photographic style, 8
Pittsburgh Courier, 18. *See also* black press
Plessy, Homer Adolph, 17
Plessy v. Ferguson, 17, 36, 37
Podis, Jennifer, 81
police dogs. *See* Birmingham, Alabama: protest movement in
Postiglione, Joseph, 77
Prince, Cecil, Neshoba County deputy, 95–97, 112
Princeton, West Virginia, 45
Pulitzer, Joseph, 19

Queens College, New York, 85

race riots, 81, 95, 96

Raeburn, John, 23
Raidford, Leigh, 3, 108
Rainey, Lawrence, Neshoba County sheriff, 95–97, 112
Randolph, A. Philip, 91
Randolph School, Topeka, Kansas, 37
Reed, Betty Jean, 70
Reeb, James, 102
Reed, Bill, 95
Richmond, Virginia, 44, 68, 73
Ritter, Norman, 77
Roberts, Eugene Leslie "Gene," Jr., 2, 17, 43, 65, 67, 92, 98, 102, 112
Roberts v. the City of Boston, 37
Robinson, Gus, 43
Roosevelt, Franklin D., 20
Rose, Gillian Rosemary, 5, 35, 110
Rosenwald Fund (*also known* as the Julius Rosenwald Fund), 13, 29n4
Rowan, Roy, 66
Russell, Richard, Georgia senator, 94
Russell, R. R., Jr., 72
Rustin, Bayard, 91

Sandeen, Eric J., 39
Sanders, Walter, 76
Schapiro, Steve, 85, 92, 102, 105n26
Schlesinger, Authur, Jr., 88
school integration, 3, 10, 17, 28, 33–38, 43–44, 53, 55, 60–68, 69, 79, 94, 108, 110–111, 115. *See also* Central High School; Harding High School; Hoxie, Arkansas; Meredith, James; University of Mississippi
Schulke, Flip, 2, 79, 81, 90–91, 108, 113
Schutzer, Paul, 70, 105n26
Schwerner, Michael, 85–86, 95, 112, 114
segregated space, 6, 17
"separate but equal," 17
Selma, Alabama, 99–102, 112; King, Martin Luther jailed in, 97–98; march to Montgomery from, 2
Sentman, Mary Alice, 21
Sibley, David, 71
sit-ins, 74, 76; Greensboro, 72; Jacksonville, Florida, 75, 94; Oklahoma City, 69; Portsmouth, Virginia, 73

Sixteenth Street Baptist Church (Birmingham, Alabama), bombing of, 93, 107
Skewes, James B., 97
slave auction, 47. *See also* Charleston, South Carolina
Smith, Brenda Lee, 69
Smith, Eugene, 71
Smith, Linda Brown, 94. *See also* Brown, Linda
Smith, Ron, 20
Smith, W. Eugene, 8
Sochurek, Howard, 44
Southern Christian Leadership Conference (SCLC), 100
Sports Illustrated magazine, 26
Steichen, Edward, 38
Stolley, Richard B., 26, 40, 47, 53–54, 60, 108, 109, 113–114
Stryker, Roy Emerson, 13–16
Student Nonviolent Coordinating Committee (SNCC), 100
Sturgis, Kentucky, 44, 62, 66
Swanberg, William Andrew, 27

Tallahatchie River, 40
Talmadge, Herman, Georgia govenor, 36
television: power of, 112; rise of, 60, 112
Tennessee State University, 52
Tenney, Gordon, 34, 105n26
Thompson, James G., 19
Thornton, Albert Sr., 52
Thornton, E. J., 52
Till-Mobley, Mamie. *See* Bradley, Mamie
Till, Louis Emmett, 28, 38, 43, 75, 111; lynching of, 34; trial, 40–42
Time magazine, 12n40, 20, 26, 27, 59, 82n4, 95, 108, 115
Tinsley, Ruth, 73, 74
Townsend, Jimmy Lee, 97
Trailways bus, 78, 111
Tri-State Defender, 59, 67. *See also* black press
Tucker, Herman, 97
Tyner, James A., 6, 18, 61, 86, 88, 99, 110

Uhrbrock, Don, 78
United Press International (UPI), 64
University of Alabama, 43
University of Mississippi riots, 10, 55, 61, 79–81, 111
University of Toledo (Ohio), 54

Van Buren High School, Arkansas, 69
Villet, Grey, 43, 46
Virginia Commonwealth University, Richmond, Virginia, 73
Voting Rights Act of 1965, 4, 81, 97, 102

Wallace, George, Alabama governor, 93
Wallace, Robert, 52
Washburn, Patrick S., 19. *See also* black press
Washington, D.C., 13, 68
Washington Post, 115
Watson, Ella, 13–16
Watts, California, riots in, 95, 97, 103–104

Wayman, Stan, 62, 66, 70; photograph by, 63
Weill, Susan M., 97
Welky, David, 21, 24
Wexler, Sanford, 91, 100
White Citizens Council, 63
whiteness, 7, 17, 49, 61, 109
Williams, Garth, 71
Williams, Hosea, 100
Wilson, L. Alex, 59, 67, 68
Wingo, Hal, 107, 113, 114
Winston-Salem, North Carolina, 66
Womack, Jacqueline, 37
Woodruff, Robert, 98
Woolworth department store, 72
Wright, Richard Nathaniel, 15

yellow journalism, 19

Zuilen, A. J., 60, 112
Zwerg, James, 77

About the Author

Michael DiBari Jr. is a photographer and educator living in Norfolk, Virginia. Before earning his master's degree in Visual Communications and Ph.D. in Journalism at Ohio University, he worked as an editorial photographer for many years. He was a staff photographer at *The Albuquerque Journal* and freelanced for publications such as *The Washington Post*, *The Los Angeles Times*, and *The Baltimore Sun* as well as the Associated Press.

He is currently the Scripps Howard Endowed Professor at the Scripps Howard School of Journalism and Communications at Hampton University.